Saving Place

50 Years of New York City Landmarks

Saving Place

50 Years of New York City Landmarks

Edited by
DONALD ALBRECHT AND ANDREW S. DOLKART WITH SERI WORDEN

Essays by
FRANÇOISE ASTORG BOLLACK
CLAUDETTE BRADY
ADELE CHATFIELD-TAYLOR
ANDREW S. DOLKART
ROBERT A.M. STERN
ANTHONY C. WOOD

Photographic Portfolios by
IWAN BAAN

Museum of the City of New York
The Monacelli Press

Published on the occasion of the exhibition
Saving Place: 50 Years
of New York City Landmarks
at the Museum of the City of New York
April 21–September 13, 2015

Copyright © 2015 Museum of the
City of New York and The Monacelli Press
Photographs © 2015 Iwan Baan

First published in the United States by
The Monacelli Press.

Library of Congress Control Number:
2015930888

ISBN 978-158093-431-2

FRONTISPIECE
Grand Central Terminal,
Park Avenue and East 42nd Street, Reed & Stem and
Warren & Wetmore, 1913,
designated 1967, interior
designated 1980

Design by Pentagram

The Monacelli Press
236 West 27th Street
New York, New York 10001

Printed in Canada

CONTENTS

FOREWORD

For those of us in the preservation trenches in the early days—I became involved in the early 1970s—few knew how revolutionary the new landmarks law was. At that time New York faced many, many challenges, including whether or not the concept of cities was obsolete. John V. Lindsay, in whose administration I served, was, however, a tremendous advocate for New York's urbanism, and he embraced preservation as a major remedy for saving the city. New York City needed saving? Was it ever possible that our city needed saving? In the 1970s, the answer was yes.

After my time in the Lindsay administration, working on the preservation of the then vacant US Custom House on Bowling Green, among other projects, I headed the newly created New York Landmarks Conservancy, whose mission was to do all things to save an important or architecturally significant building, including ownership and leaseholds—through any legal arrangement. The Landmarks Conservancy was a creation of the Municipal Art Society, as were the Historic Districts Council and the Friends of the Upper East Side, to name only a few. To this day, these city-wide groups and a host of other preservation organizations have fought with city hall and, frequently, they have won.

The early activists who advocated for preservation were urban pioneers. They include Joan Davidson and the J. M. Kaplan Fund, Margot Gayle, Brendan Gill, Otis Pratt Pearsall, Terry Benbow, Barbaralee Diamonstein, Whitney North Seymour Sr., Fred Papert, Simon Breines, Donald Oresman, and, above all, Kent Barwick. They did make the saving of New York possible, with preservation of landmarks and whole neighborhoods key factors in the rebirth of the city in the final quarter of the twentieth century.

Within the newly formed Landmarks Preservation Commission, those who guided and preserved the law in the early days were Chairmen Harmon Goldstone and Geoffrey Platt, and, as counsel for many years, Dorothy Miner. A very able lawyer, Dorothy was a fierce advocate who led the crafting of the winning arguments for both Penn Central and St. Bartholomew's Church.

For my part, I personally dedicate this book to all of them.

Saving Place: 50 Years of New York's Landmarks became a project of the City Museum at the urging of ex-officio trustee and then chairman of the Landmarks Preservation Commission, Robert B. Tierney, and Anthony C. Wood, chairman of the New York Preservation Archive Project. But the group who made the project a reality was a committee of co-chairs, and I thank each and every one of them: Frederick Bland, Jim Hanley, Hugh Hardy, William Higgins, John J. Kerr, Richard Olcott, Raymond Pepi, Frank Sciame, and Robert B. Tierney. I also salute all the chairs of the Landmarks Preservation Commission who lent their names as Honorary Chairs: Kent Barwick, Laurie Beckelman, Gene Norman, Sherida Paulsen, Jennifer Raab, Beverly Moss Spatt, Meenakshi Srinivasan, and Robert B. Tierney.

The exhibition has been skillfully realized by curators Donald Albrecht, the City Museum's curator of Architecture and Design, and Andrew S. Dolkart, director of the Historic Preservation Program at Columbia University's Graduate School of Architecture, Planning, and Preservation. They were ably assisted by Seri Worden, associate curator. I also want to thank all the institutions and individuals who lent materials to the exhibition. The design of *Saving Place* has been undertaken with great style by architect Wendy Evans Joseph, head of Studio Joseph; graphic designer Jacob Wildschiødtz and his team from NR2154; and lighting designer Anita Jorgensen of Anita Jorgensen Lighting Design.

In addition to their efforts, I acknowledge the book's authors as well as its designers, Michael Bierut and Laitsz Ho of Pentagram, and photographer Iwan Baan, whom the City Museum commissioned to create a portfolio of new photographs of individual landmarks and historic districts. It was also a pleasure, once again, to collaborate with Elizabeth White of The Monacelli Press.

All told, *Saving Place* underscores how civic and business leaders, grassroots activists, and design professionals have come together to create a contemporary New York City that blends old and new in a dynamic urbanism. The story of preservation is one that influences New Yorkers every day, one that is often, but should never be, taken for granted.

SUSAN HENSHAW JONES
RONAY MENSCHEL DIRECTOR, MUSEUM OF THE CITY OF NEW YORK

SAVING PLACE: 50 YEARS OF NEW YORK CITY LANDMARKS

THIS BOOK AND A COMPANION EXHIBITION ARE MADE POSSIBLE BY

CO-CHAIRS

Frederick Bland
Jim Hanley
Hugh Hardy
William Higgins
John J. Kerr, Esq.
Richard Olcott
Raymond Pepi
Frank Sciame
Robert B. Tierney

HONORARY CO-CHAIRS

Kent Barwick
Laurie Beckelman
Gene Norman
Sherida Paulsen
Jennifer Raab
Beverly Moss Spatt
Meenakshi Srinivasan
Robert B. Tierney

CO-SPONSORS

New York City Landmarks Preservation
    Commission
The Architectural League of New York
Historic Districts Council
The Municipal Art Society
The New York Landmarks Conservancy
New York Landmarks Preservation
    Foundation
The New York Preservation Archive Project

DONORS

J.M. Kaplan Fund
Con Edison
Extell Development Company
Robert A. and Elizabeth R. Jeffe Foundation
New York Landmarks Preservation
    Foundation
Sciame/Frank Sciame
Taconic Builders/Jim Hanley
Two Trees Management Company/
    David Walentas

42nd Street Development Corporation
Allade
O. Kelley Anderson
Beyer Blinder Belle
The Brodsky Organization

Carolyn S. Brody Family Foundation
Capalino+Company
David F. and Frances A. Eberhart Foundation
Ennead Architects
John J. Kerr and Nora Wren Kerr
L & L Holding Company
New York Preservation Archive Project
Peter Pennoyer Architects
Reilly Windows & Doors/Michael Reilly
Robert A.M. Stern Architects
Howard L. Zimmerman Architects

Artistic Doors & Windows Manufacturing
Authentic Window Design
Bentel & Bentel, Architects/Planners
BKSK Architects

Françoise Bollack and Thomas Killian

Bone Levine Architects

Brisk Waterproofing Company

Building Conservation Associates/
    Raymond M. Pepi

Catherine Cahill and William Bernhard

Carnegie Hill Neighbors

Center Development Corporation/
    William Hubbard

COOKFOX

Anne Covell and William Higgins

Suzanne Davis and Rolf Ohlhausen

Deerpath Construction Corporation

Ferguson & Shamamian Architects

H3 Hardy Collaboration Architecture/
    Hugh Hardy

Higgins Quasebarth & Partners

William and Robin D. Hubbard

Ingram Yuzek Gainen Carroll & Bertolotti

E. William Judson

Stephen S. Lash

Brenda Levin

Empire State Realty Trust

James Marston Fitch Charitable Foundation

Murphy Burnham & Buttrick Architects

The Nanz Company

Old Structures Engineering

Thomas Phifer and Partners

Platt Byard Dovell White Architects

Polart Group/Wesley Armatowski

Lee Harris Pomeroy Architects

Encarnita and Robert Quinlan

G.P. Schafer Architect

SHoP Architects

Skyline Windows/Peter Warren

Barbara and Donald Tober Foundation

Cynthia Wainwright and Stephen Berger

West New York Restoration of CT

Roy J. Zuckerberg Family Foundation/
    Lloyd Zuckerberg

Mr. and Mrs. Oscar K. Anderson III

Patricia Begley and George H. Beane

Stephen G. Berliner/Savills Studley

Lucienne and Claude Bloch

Joan H. Geismar, Ph.D.

Jeanne Giordano and Robert Frasca

Linda Yowell Architects

Nicholson & Galloway

Nancy and Otis Pearsall

Nicholas Quennell

Annabelle Selldorf

WITH PUBLIC SUPPORT FROM

Honorable Speaker Melissa Mark-Viverito
    City Council
Honorable Helen Rosenthal
    City Council Member
New York State Council on the Arts

List as of February 20, 2015.

PAGES **10–11** Manhattan, looking south toward New York Harbor and Staten Island

PAGES **12–13** Manhattan, Upper East Side, with Fifth Avenue and the Metropolitan Museum of Art

ROBERT A.M. STERN

Introduction

Fifty years have passed since the New York City Landmarks Law was introduced as a powerful force in the evolution of New York's architecture, urbanism, and real estate. Much of what we love about New York today we owe to the law and its administering body. Much of what is contentious about contemporary development and redevelopment can also be laid at the feet of the landmarks law and the Landmarks Preservation Commission, which, with regard to the execution of its mandate, is frequently inconsistent, sometimes capricious, sometimes susceptible to trendiness, and quite often politically motivated.

The Landmarks Preservation Commission was born out of destruction in 1965: the demolition two years earlier of McKim, Mead & White's Pennsylvania Station, an unwitting sacrifice that shook New Yorkers into action. Historic preservation as a legislative concept was pretty much an innovation to New Yorkers, but the act of preservation itself was a different story. For nearly two centuries, grassroots activists and civic groups had worked to safeguard New York's architectural treasures, but with no legal footing to combat the jug-gernaut of "progress." With the passage of the landmarks law, a jolt was sent through the city's real estate ecosystem. A formidable new member of the food chain, long in gestation, had now arrived, and it was one to be reckoned with. All the players—property owners, developers, politicians, lawyers, architects, and citizens alike—were sent scrambling to adjust to the new rules. A cottage

East 64th Street between Park and Lexington Avenues, show-ing Russell Sage Foundation and Robert Sterling Clark Foundation (originally Asia House), Philip Johnson, 1960, and, right, townhouse, Agrest and Gandelsonas Architects, 1984, Upper East Side Historic District, designated 1981

industry of consultants was born—which over time has grown to mansion proportions.

Contrary to what might have been expected, the law didn't spawn a preservation land grab. With the exception of the Brooklyn Heights Historic District, comprising 1,300 buildings and recognized as a National Register Historic Landmark seven months before becoming the city's first historic district in November 1965, early designations were fine-tuned, focusing on obvious—very old or "safe"—buildings as well as on historic districts often no larger than a city block or two. After a few years, that laser focus was widened to a floodlight: the Greenwich Village Historic District was designated in 1969 with approximately 2,000 buildings, the substantial Cobble Hill District followed that year in Brooklyn, and the Park Slope and SoHo–Cast Iron Districts protected large areas in 1973. By necessity much of the early work was preservation triage, the result of frantic efforts to protect against imminent threats. As a growing number of neighborhood-based advocacy groups, along with newly determined citizens, became more driven and proactive, being "at risk" was no longer the principal motivation for landmarks consideration.

The designation of historic districts is perhaps the law's most essential power, for protecting the fabric of the city—not just the foreground architectural icons but the "everyday masterpieces," the modestly scaled background structures that are vital to rounding out a full picture of the city's past—is central to effective preservation. Paul Rudolph, my teacher at Yale, said that modern architects could design individual iconic buildings but were unable to design the background buildings so critical to the texture of the city. This is just as true now, in this age when too many architects and their clients are unable to get over the narcissism of the self-important project, so that the fabric of the city is frequently demeaned and its preservation is more important than ever.

Fifty years on, the landmarks law has become a decisive factor in the city's physical and social history. But most surprisingly and most significantly, it has become a formidable planning tool in its own right. Historic preservation is not the rather esoteric pursuit it once seemed to be. It is a powerful, entrenched political force, not only in New York but throughout the country, with an ethos and a sophisticated means for lobbying, the magnitude of which no one expected.

The big landmarks questions from the first have been significance, which can be architectural, historical, or cultural, and the repurposing of old buildings. Because the contemporary world of aesthetics is not governed by an accepted canon, beauty, which might be a key criterion of significance, gives way to its watered-down sibling, "appropriateness," a vague term dictating what is allowed, aesthetically, to be inflicted upon landmarked buildings by way of so-called adaptive reuse and on landmark settings by way of the idea of zeitgeist, or the need for contemporary expression. "Significance" must be continually confronted and redefined. History teaches us that the art of the recent past is usually viewed with disdain, so we have to be sure to hold on to as much of the recent past as we can, making sure that it is still with us when it returns to fashion. An earlier generation abhorred so-called Victorian architecture. Today, many find it difficult to appreciate stylistic modernism, perhaps understandably so, since modernism was the nemesis of the preservation movement in the early 1960s, when its proponents were largely to blame for the senseless bulldozing of many fine old buildings to make way for cheaply constructed, crudely conceived new ones.

Trying to get past this particular prejudice, in 1996, I brought attention to thirty-five modernist landmarks-in-waiting, works that were eligible or soon to be eligible for designation but which, for largely aesthetic reasons grounded in disdain for the recent past, were not protected. Now, almost twenty years later, it is somewhat comforting to report that thirteen of these buildings have been landmarked, but very unfortunately three have been demolished or otherwise remodeled beyond recognition, and the fates of the rest hang precariously in the balance. Some, such as Lincoln Center (1962–68) have, for the most part, been creatively altered, though at some sacrifice to the cohesion of the ensemble. Irving Fenichel's Knickerbocker Laundry (1932), in Queens, has seen its architectural character dramatically transformed to something that may enjoy landmark status in the future as a digitally designed church, but now looks pretty awkward to many of us. Philip Johnson's New York State Pavilion (1964), despite substantial publicity and revitalization efforts, remains undesignated and in near ruin.

I'm pleased that so many of the buildings on my list are now protected, but the losses have been painful. Victor Lundy's Church of the Resurrection (1965), 325 East 101st Street in East Harlem, was torn down in 2009 to make way for the construction of an apartment building. Edgar I. Williams's quietly dignified Donnell Library (1955), opposite the Museum of Modern Art on West 53rd Street, was demolished in 2011 to make way for a high-rise hotel. The saddest loss, Edward Durell Stone's 1964 Gallery of Modern Art, 2 Columbus Circle, built for A&P supermarket heir Huntington Hartford, was also the most confounding. Despite vigorous arguments from New Yorkers both within and outside of the architecture community, the Landmarks Preservation Commission—in perhaps the most egregious of its periodic failures—never calendared the building. Now gutted and reskinned as the Museum of Arts and Design, only its distinct massing remains as a bitter reminder of what was lost.

Even as we gradually come to terms with the architecture of modernism, what stubbornly lingers is the psychology of modernism, the outmoded belief that the past is not worth knowing, let alone preserving, and that historic preservation is somehow a hindrance to progress and a sop to the sentimental. This couldn't be further from the truth. The city's historic fabric is what makes New York relevant, livable, and distinct, creating value, stability, and a sense of time and place. The fact that historic preservation reinforces these qualities, that it is a vitalizing force in neighborhoods, is insufficiently recognized.

The real estate community is not wrong when it describes the creation of historic districts as backdoor physical planning. Even though their cries of foul sometimes seem more like the howls of hungry wolves, they certainly have a point. But so what? Absent a strong physical planning process, the preservation of historic neighborhoods has done wonders to rejuvenate many parts of the city. Downzoning or creating districts such as the Special Clinton Zoning District, where the height of new development is based on its immediate context, can both preserve the scale that is so important to the character of a neighborhood and disincentivize developers who will look to other areas for greater return. But this approach doesn't sufficiently address the character of a neighborhood that arises from an aesthetic dialogue that comes when buildings in a given area speak to each other in aesthetic terms. Historic district designation has time and time again—in the SoHo, Ladies' Mile, and Gansevoort Market Districts, to name just a few—provided a reassuring sense that an area has a stable future, thereby encouraging reinvestment.

Quite possibly, in the 1960s, some preservationists in our city saw the movement as an endgame, with a limited number of examples to be designated. But, to the chagrin of many, the preservation movement is open-ended. Every year brings new possibilities as another crop of buildings turns thirty. And it is not only individual buildings that acquire significance, or even neighborhoods, but all kinds of structures that are landmarks in every sense of the word. On Coney Island, we've protected the Cyclone roller coaster, the Parachute Jump, and the Wonder Wheel. The Unisphere, a relic from the 1964–65 World's Fair in Flushing Meadows–Corona Park, Queens, was designated in 1995. And there are roughly one hundred landmarked street lampposts and seven cast-iron street clocks throughout the city. Advertising signs seem to be the next target for preservation, recalling the industrial heritage of areas in which manufacturing is all but lost, and also reflecting the fact that bold graphics are an art form that gives many people visual pleasure and a sense of place. Public sentiment in favor of Long Island City's iconic Pepsi-Cola sign, long poised atop a bottling plant, led to its retention when the site was redeveloped. Likewise, the Domino Sugar sign that announced a refinery on the Williamsburg waterfront is to survive the near wholesale demolition of the complex, albeit in a polished new setting where its industrial heft is sure to be diminished. The eight-story Kentile Floors sign that until recently stood high in the Gowanus sky has been dismantled, but again owing to public sentiment, saved for future reconstruction. Such components of the built environment have just as much meaning to many New Yorkers as buildings and monuments. We have to take them seriously.

As preservation moves forward, stewardship is perhaps the issue most in crisis. We have become too lenient about the change that is allowed to take place to landmark buildings and districts. In some cases the culprit is surely the commission's workload. With a team of roughly seventy responsible for thousands of applications each year, ranging from the mundane to the mammoth, the commission is chronically understaffed and underfunded. Mistakes are made, buildings are lost to oversight, to bureaucratic lapses, to short-circuited communication between the commission and other agencies, such as the Buildings Department. In one of the more mind-bending and ultimately disheartening bureaucratic snafus, the Cathedral Church of St. John the Divine was granted landmark status in 2003 but the City Council quickly overturned it, arguing that even greater protection was warranted—that not only the church itself but also its surrounding campus, including additional structures, merited designation. The mayor vetoed the council's action, but the council overrode the veto and the LPC did not revisit the issue, leaving both church and campus vulnerable to the destructive forces of development that have now begun to severely compromise what is an incomparable New York setting.

More often than through an administrative blunder, landmarks are compromised by the commission's subjective aesthetic determination that an architectural intervention is acceptable, decisions that are colored by the politics of taste, not to mention politics pure and simple. Preservationists like to reassure the doubting public that landmark designation will not freeze the city in amber, that it allows—and simply curates—change. Yes, buildings must adapt, but there is a difference between accommodating change and approving desecration. We need keystone cops, not Keystone Cops. More and more, the commission seems to lose track of the original asset for which it is responsible. The preservation community itself is more fragmented than it ought to be, with groups myopically advocating for their own causes but failing to show solidarity when it is needed.

Despite fifty years of progress, historic preservation faces as many obstacles as ever. Prized buildings and neighborhoods continue to slip through our fingers, the victims of economic and political pressures and mere oversight. Adaptive reuse is an indispensable weapon in the preservation arsenal, but it is difficult to convey the aura of the past once a building or a neighborhood has lost its original function, once it awakens, like Rip Van Winkle, in a new time. It is a perpetual challenge to maintain a sense of authenticity and there is no clear formula, but the first step must be to respect the buildings we have moved to protect. Gaining landmark status is only the beginning of the story— maintaining those protections to the highest standards is crucial.

At the fifty-year mark, the landmarks law has seen its fair share of life's moments—growing pains, grand ambitions, heartaches, health scares, proud achievements, and controversies. It may be in a perpetual state of crisis, but it is not yet at midlife; its directive is clear, and its place and importance in the context of New York is well established. Nonetheless, it is important that we now, as this book seeks to do, take stock, redouble our efforts, and get back to the ideals that inspired the small band of picketers who marched in front of a threatened Pennsylvania Station a half century ago.

Written with Jacob Tilove

Manhattan

PAGES 22–23 AND 24–25
Castle Clinton, Battery Park,
Lt. Col. Jonathan Williams
and John McComb Jr., 1811,
designated 1965

26 Saving Place

OPPOSITE Foley Square,
showing New York State
Supreme Court (originally New
York County Courthouse), Guy
Lowell, 1927, designated 1966
and, right, Thurgood Marshall
United States Courthouse
(originally United States
Courthouse), Cass Gilbert
and Cass Gilbert Jr., 1936,
designated 1975

ABOVE Municipal Building,
1 Centre Street, McKim, Mead
& White, 1914, designated 1966

City Hall, City Hall Park,
Joseph-François Mangin
and John McComb Jr., 1811,
designated 1966

PAGES **30–31** Manhattan,
looking southeast with the East
River in the distance

ABOVE Broome Street, SoHo–Cast Iron Historic District, designated 1973

OPPOSITE ABOVE Spring Street, SoHo–Cast Iron Historic District

OPPOSITE BELOW Prince Street, SoHo–Cast Iron Historic District

PAGES 34–35 The facade of 51 Astor Place (Fumihiko Maki, 2013) reflects 770 Broadway, (originally Wanamaker's Department Store), Daniel H. Burnham, 1907, NoHo Historic District, designated 2000. At right, The Cooper Union, Frederick A. Peterson, 1859, designated 1965

PAGES 36–37 Astor Place. From left, The Cooper Union, Frederick A. Peterson, 1859, designated 1965, 445 Lafayette Street (outside the historic district), Gwathmey Siegel Architects, 2006, Joseph Papp Public Theater (originally Astor Library), Alexander Saeltzer, Griffith Thomas, Thomas Stent, 1849–81, designated 1965 and now in the NoHo Historic District

PAGES **38–39** Jefferson
Market Branch, New York
Public Library (originally
Jefferson Market Courthouse),
Sixth Avenue and West 10th
Street, Vaux & Withers, 1877,   ABOVE AND OPPOSITE
Greenwich Village Historic   Jefferson Market Branch, New
District, designated 1969   York Public Library

40 Saving Place

ANTHONY C. WOOD

Origins of the Landmarks Law

Today New York City's landmarks and historic districts are such an accepted and expected part of the cityscape that many present-day New Yorkers take them for granted. However, the survival of these landmarks is anything but accidental. The year 2015 marks the fiftieth anniversary of the passage of the law that declared as matter of public policy that preservation of New York's landmarks was a "necessity" and established a legal public process to ensure their survival would not be left to chance.

New York's landmarks law was not the product of a top-down government mandate but rather the creation of an engaged and impassioned citizenry tired of losing their city's historic, architectural, and cultural treasures. New Yorkers demanded a public process that would give them a formal opportunity to save the city's landmarks. It is because of decades of their civic activism, persistence, and creativity that New York has its landmarks law.

The landmarks law can be seen as the confluence of two streams of nineteenth-century thought and action: the concern for preserving the historic and a belief in the importance of the aesthetic. The historic motivation has its roots in the nineteenth-century movement to preserve places with patriotic associations. Illustrative of such efforts are the 1850 purchase by New York State of Washington's headquarters in Newburgh as the country's first historic house museum and the legendary work in 1853 to preserve Mount Vernon by Anne

Jefferson Market Branch, New York Public Library (originally Jefferson Market Courthouse), Sixth Avenue and West 10th Street, Vaux & Withers, 1877, Greenwich Village Historic District, designated 1969

Pamela Cunningham and her Mount Vernon Ladies' Association of the Union. Most famously beating the drum for preservation in New York was Andrew Haswell Green and his American Scenic and Historic Preservation Society.

The other motivational force, the focus on the aesthetic, came from the City Beautiful Movement. Inspired by the World's Columbian Exposition of 1893, scores of influential New Yorkers returned home from Chicago with visions of what a great city could be. They funneled their energy and civic passion into the creation and operation of art societies. For the history of preservation, the most important of these was the Municipal Art Society, founded in 1893.

Edward Lamson Henry, *St. John's Park and Chapel*, 1905

LEFT St. John's
Park and Chapel,
Varick, Laight and
Beach Streets, John
McComb Jr. and
Isaac McComb,
1803, demolished,
1918

BELOW Billboards
on Fifth Avenue
between East
89th and 90th
Streets, from the
Report of the
Mayor's Billboard
Advertising
Commission, 1913

Robert Moses and
a model of Lower
Manhattan showing
the proposed
Brooklyn-Battery
Bridge, 1939

The early 1900s saw a number of preservation efforts in New York City involving such historic sites as the Morris-Jumel Mansion and Fraunces Tavern and multi-year struggles over City Hall and St. John's Chapel. As important as these efforts were, the earliest cause that had a direct influence on the creation of New York's law was an aesthetic issue: the visual pollution of rampant advertising on Fifth Avenue. By 1913 the concern over this flood of advertising compelled Mayor William J. Gaynor to appoint the Billboard Advertising Commission of the City of New York to study the problem. Providing funding to support this effort were both the American Scenic and Historic Preservation Society and the Municipal Art Society. After public hearings and much research, the commission concluded that the city was powerless to meaningfully address the issue. The key proposal was an amendment to the New York State Constitution that would empower cities to regulate on the grounds of aesthetics. The driving force behind this recommendation was civic activist and lawyer Albert Sprague Bard.

It was not until 1954 that the Supreme Court in *Berman v. Parker* affirmed that cities had the right to regulate private property on the grounds of aesthetics. This helps explain why despite efforts by Bard and a cadre of civic organizations, the amendment failed to gain traction at the 1915 New York State Constitutional Convention. Repackaged by Bard as the "patrimony of the people" amendment for consideration at the 1938 convention, the concept was still decades ahead of the times. Undaunted, Bard would continue to explore mechanisms to regulate private property to protect the "natural beauty, historic associations, sightlines and physical good order of the state and its parts." Events shortly following the 1938 Convention would help convince New York's civic community of the pressing need for a legal mechanism to provide an orderly process to preserve New York's architectural, historical, and cultural assets.

The excesses of Robert Moses, the immensely powerful and then-popular public figure who simultaneously held multiple governmental positions involving land use, planning, and parks, provided this wake-up call. In January 1939 Moses unveiled plans for the Brooklyn-Battery Bridge. In vintage Moses style, he sought to steamroll the proposal through the approval processes. What Moses saw as a gleaming modern addition to the city many civic leaders saw as disfiguring the face of Lower Manhattan, which the Fine Arts Federation called, "the most thrillingly beautiful and world-renowned feature of this great city." Brutally attacking his prominent civic opponents, deftly playing his political cards, and taking no prisoners, Moses rammed the project through. Only the behind-the-scenes intervention of President Franklin D. Roosevelt stopped the project.

The bridge plan was quickly replaced with a proposed tunnel. Despite extensive evidence to the contrary, a vindictive Moses insisted that the new tunnel required the demolition of the beloved Castle Clinton. At this point in its long life, the Castle was functioning as the highly popular New York Aquarium. A coalition of civic groups even more diverse than that forged to battle the bridge took up arms. The siege of the Castle would last a decade. Again existing public processes, reasoned arguments, and expert evidence could not stand up to the raw wielding of power by Moses. Again external forces intervened: the outbreak of World War II and the resulting shortage of heavy equipment, which was required to demolish the Castle's eight-foot-plus-thick walls, gave its defenders the time to devise and implement a preservation strategy for the site.

These two battles with Moses, one over aesthetics and the other over a historic site, were not isolated incidents. Other threats to historic resources by Moses, combined with an acute awareness of losses during the early years of the war in Europe, launched a nascent effort in 1941 by the Municipal Art Society and other organizations to explore a mechanism to protect New York's historic and architectural treasures. Ironically the war saved Castle Clinton, but it derailed this early effort to devise a system to protect the city's landmarks.

The postwar period brought huge pressure on the built fabric of the city: highways, high-rises, institutional expansions, Robert Moses, and a populace increasingly entranced by the romance of the new, accelerated change. The historic neighborhoods of Brooklyn Heights and Greenwich Village were particularly threatened and would become bastions of preservation. Midtown Manhattan was experiencing the loss of buildings never before thought to be in danger; the Ritz-Carlton Hotel and the Collegiate Church of St. Nicholas yielded to the wrecker's ball.

In 1950 the president of the Municipal Art Society publicly called for a landmarks law. Three elements needed to be in place to achieve this goal: an inventory of sites that such a law should protect, an articulate constituency to help create the political will to pass such a law, and lastly a legal basis for the regulation of private property on aesthetic grounds. Thanks to dedicated citizens, neighborhood organizations, civic and professional organizations, and the continuing relentless assault on the city's historic fabric, this tripartite agenda gradually advanced.

Working with the Society of Architectural Historians, the Municipal Art Society released a preliminary inventory of buildings worthy of protection, a list that was refined during the 1950s and provided the intellectual capital for a series of efforts to educate the public and alert it to what was at risk. Exhibitions, walking tours, and a plaque program were among the initatives that helped to expand the preservation constituency beyond the highly visible controversies in Greenwich Village and Brooklyn Heights.

In 1954 plans to demolish Grand Central Terminal were announced. Acting on his strong personal conviction that government did have the right to regulate private property on aesthetic grounds, Albert Bard drafted authorizing legislation that would give New York City that power. Bard's long-held belief received a great boost when shortly thereafter the Supreme Court issued its decision in *Berman v. Parker*, providing support for Bard's assertion. The Bard Act, as it would come to be known, was introduced in Albany in 1955 by State Senator McNeil Mitchell. On its second try, with support from an array of New York civic groups, the National Trust for Historic Preservation, and the mayor of New York, the Act became law in April 1956.

A legal basis for New York City to devise a formal process to protect its landmarks was finally in place. So why did it take almost another decade for New York City to use that authority to pass its landmarks law? Civic groups realized the possibilities of the Bard Act, as did grassroots preservationists in Brooklyn Heights and Greenwich Village. Citing the Bard Act, Brooklyn activists went so far as to draft their own version of a landmarks law to protect Brooklyn Heights. Villagers, who for decades had been seeking some sort of landmarks protection, recognized the power of the Bard Act and launched a petition drive urging its use. Bard, then ninety-two, was the first of 10,000 signatories to the petition.

These efforts to use the Bard Act as the basis for passing either historic zoning or a freestanding landmarks law to protect threatened buildings and neighborhoods, would ultimately hit an unmovable roadblock. In July 1956, the new chairman of the New York City Planning Commission, James Felt, announced his ambitious, politically daunting, and multiyear plan to rewrite the city's zoning resolution. Initially, it was hoped this process might provide the platform for advancing landmark protection through historic zoning. Ultimately Felt concluded that trying to address the landmark issue within the new zoning resolution was too politically risky. He promised the preservation advo-

LEFT Ritz-Carlton
Hotel, Madison
Avenue between
46th and 47th
Streets, Warren
& Wetmore, 1911,
demolished 1951

RIGHT Albert S.
Bard, 1961

cates that he would address their issue after the passage of his new zoning. The result was more frustrating years of threatened and lost landmarks.

By 1961, with his new zoning accomplished, Felt was ready to deliver on his promise. In the interim the city had lived through a number of preservation dramas. The Jefferson Market Courthouse and Carnegie Hall were saved, and a proposal for bowling alleys in the interior of Grand Central had been fought off. Central Park remained under assault by the proposed 1,000-seat Huntington Hartford Café. Greenwich Village and Brooklyn Heights were living under constant threats. Political will to do something was building.

True to his word, Felt helped advance the landmark agenda. Working closely with such civic leaders as Geoffrey Platt and Harmon Goldstone, Felt orchestrated Mayor Wagner's creation of the Committee for the Preservation of Structures of Historic and Esthetic Importance. Based on the committee's recommendations, the mayor appointed the first Landmarks Preservation Commission on April 21, 1962. It was tasked with identifying and designating historic sites and drafting a landmarks law, but it had no legal authority to protect anything.

While these governmental advances were being made, New Yorkers continued to see buildings threatened and witnessed the demolition of others.

Since the 1950s, with various proposals for its replacement having been floated, Pennsylvania Station had been dodging its date with the demolition crew. That threat became real again when plans for a new terminal were revealed in the summer of 1961. At that moment the established civic organizations were working with the Wagner administration and the new commission to obtain a law that would provide legal authority to protect landmarks. Taking an aggressive posture against the demolition of Pennsylvania Station could have put that effort in jeopardy. McKim, Mead & White's massive Beaux-Arts marvel was in the way of a $120 million project promising to produce $5 million in tax revenues, employ a small army, and replace a then-down-at-the-heels train station with a brand-new Madison Square Garden, exhibit hall, and thirty-three-story

ABOVE LEFT
Giorgio Cavaglieri,
perspective of the
Jefferson Market
Branch, New York
Public Library, 1961

ABOVE RIGHT
Margot Gayle,
a leader in the
fight to save the
Jefferson Market
Courthouse

LEFT Carnegie Hall,
Seventh Avenue
and West 57th
Street, William
Burnet Tuthill, 1891

Origins of the Landmarks Law **51**

office tower. Opposing the plan could have seriously endangered the efforts to get a landmarks law passed.

Pennsylvania Station did not go down without protests, however. Partially frustrated by the timidity of the established civic organizations, Action Group for Better Architecture in New York (AGBANY) was formed by a feisty group of young architects and other concerned New Yorkers. They took to the streets. Though the ranks of those who protested against the demolition was modest by today's standards (at the most several hundred), their actions elevated the battle to a new level of public visibility. On October 28, 1963, the actual demolition began, triggering one of the most powerful preservation passages ever penned, a *New York Times* editorial authored by Ada Louise Huxtable. It concludes: "Any city gets what it admires, will pay for, and ultimately, deserves. Even when we had Penn Station, we couldn't afford to keep it clean. We want and deserve tin-can architecture in a tin-horn culture. And we will probably be judged not by the monuments we build but by those we have destroyed." The very public three-year destruction of the station, while trains kept running, would daily rub the face of countless New Yorkers in this raw wound.

The demolition of Penn Station helped to create the political will needed to advance the landmarks law. Also stirring the pot was steady press coverage

Isaac Brokaw Mansion, Fifth Avenue and East 79th Street, Rose and Stone, 1890

of such preservation dramas as the fate of the Brooklyn Savings Bank, the Custom House, and the city's oldest house, the Pieter Clasen Wyckoff home, c. 1652. Between 1961 and the passage of the landmarks law in 1965, the *New York Times* alone ran more than twenty pro-preservation editorials. Most, if not all, were written by Huxtable. Their headlines screamed, "Anything Left to Preserve?" "The Crumbling Landmarks," and "As the Wrecker's Ball Swings." They provided a steady drum beat for preservation.

A final barrage of threats and losses would propel the city to take action. By the spring of 1964, a draft landmarks law was on Mayor Wagner's desk. There it sat. In August the planned demolition of the Savoy-Plaza at Fifth Avenue and 59th Street was announced. Finally in September, in an embarrassing public relations snafu, the mayor proudly proclaimed American Landmarks Preservation Week in New York City just as the news broke that the Brokaw Mansion, a prominent baronial castle anchoring the highly visible corner of 79th Street and Fifth Avenue, was slated for demolition. The Landmarks Commission had designated the building, and it sported its landmark plaque, but neither provided it with an ounce of protection.

The Brokaw crisis moved the draft landmarks law from the mayor's desk to the New York City Council. Public rallies to save landmarks, long a staple in Greenwich Village and Brooklyn Heights, now came to the Upper East Side. The pressure was mounting. In December the City Council held its public hearing on the proposed law. There, along with more than eighty others, were repre-

Demolition of the Isaac Brokaw Mansion, 1965

sentatives of the Municipal Art Society and the American Scenic and Historic Preservation Society. They had been there at the beginning of the journey with their funding of the 1913 Mayoral Commission and had lasted to the end. Sadly, Albert Bard had not. He had died in March 1963.

Over the Christmas holidays, another highly public preservation high-wire act unfolded. Demolition began on two of the stately mansions, now known as the Pyne Davison Row, on the west side of Park Avenue between East 68th and 69th Streets. As fireplace mantels and decorative floors were being removed from 680 and 684 Park Avenue, an anonymous donor purchased the buildings. As the *New York Times* commented, "Miracles and magnanimity are fine, but they are not the legislative answer to preservation. That lies in the hands of the City Council—now." The council continued to study the draft landmarks legislation. Their work, however, would be put into high gear when late on Friday, February 8, 1965, demolition began on the Brokaw Mansion. The public outrage was palpable. The headline of the *New York Times* editorial said it all: "Rape of the Brokaw Mansion."

What would be the next loss? Singing "Where Have All the Landmarks Gone," schoolchildren marched to save the threatened Old Merchant's House. Or would it be the Friends Meeting House at 144 East 20th Street, which had just been sold to a developer? Fortunately, losing the Brokaw Mansion was enough. It was embarrassingly clear that New York's city fathers had lost control of their own city. The City Council took action, and on April 6, 1965, passed the bill. Mayor Wagner signed it on April 19. After decades of pitched preservation battles, painful losses, and cliff-hanging near misses, a legal process to protect the city's cherished buildings and historic neighborhoods was finally in place. The tireless efforts of countless individuals—some famous, many not—civic organizations (both large and small, neighborhood-based and citywide) and professional associations had finally borne fruit. Knowing this legacy is an essential prerequisite for understanding both the early application of the law during its first half century of use and preservation advocacy during that period.

One might think that the signing of the law would have been the cause of great celebration and that its passage would have unleashed a flood of unfettered preservation activity, but that was not the case. On the signing of the new law, Mayor Wagner made it clear he had heard the voices of the real estate interests who had opposed it. He publicly cautioned that if the law was found to be "too restrictive on property rights or did not meet the problems of landmarks owners" it would quickly be amended.

The fragility of the new law was not lost on the early leaders of the Landmarks Preservation Commission. Their law was untested and their agency virtually unknown. Those leading the commission were extremely conscious of the need to proceed with utmost caution. As a result, for many years the top priority of the Landmarks Preservation Commission was preserving the landmarks law itself. Underscoring this was a sign on the desk of a senior commission staff member that read, "This Law Raises Grave Constitutional Questions." All the years of effort invested in achieving the law, all the buildings that had been lost along the way, all would be for naught if the commission overreached and the law was repealed by the courts or weakened through restrictive

Metropolitan Opera House, Broadway and West 39th Street, J. C. Cady, 1883, demolished 1967

amendments at City Hall.

Cautious application of the landmarks law helped the commission establish its validity and its own bona fides. This would serve preservation well, but the strategy came at a cost. Buildings that preservation activists felt the law was created to save were lost, including such treasures as the Singer Building and the Metropolitan Opera House.

It was a threat to Grand Central Terminal that caused the commission to draw a line in the sand. If the law was unable to save that icon, then ultimately what was it worth? In 1969, with the vote to turn down the proposal to build a tower above Grand Central Terminal, the commissioners knew the landmarks law was on the line. The legal challenge would ultimately wend its way to the United States Supreme Court and the public campaign to save Grand Central received national attention. Finally, on June 26, 1978, the Supreme Court upheld New York's landmarks law, and the shadow of uncertainty that had hung over the law for almost a decade, was lifted.

When the law was passed in 1965, preservationists did not achieve all their goals. The original law did not provide for the preservation of interiors or scenic landmarks. It also burdened the commission with administrative constraints, including a moratorium on designations. These limitations were addressed in the 1973 amendments to the law. Further process changes would come with the abolition of the Board of Estimate and the redistribution of its powers to other governmental bodies through the Charter Revision of 1990.

As it should be, the primary focus of the landmark law's golden anniversary is the remarkable achievements, and at times keen disappointments, of the first fifty years of preservation under the law. Yet to fully appreciate and understand that half century, it is essential to be aware of its context: the activities of the century that preceded it. For when it comes to the history of preservation, William Faulkner's famous observation holds true: "The past is never dead. It's not even past."

This essay is based on research extensively documented in Preserving New York: Winning the Right to Protect a City's Landmarks *by Anthony C. Wood*

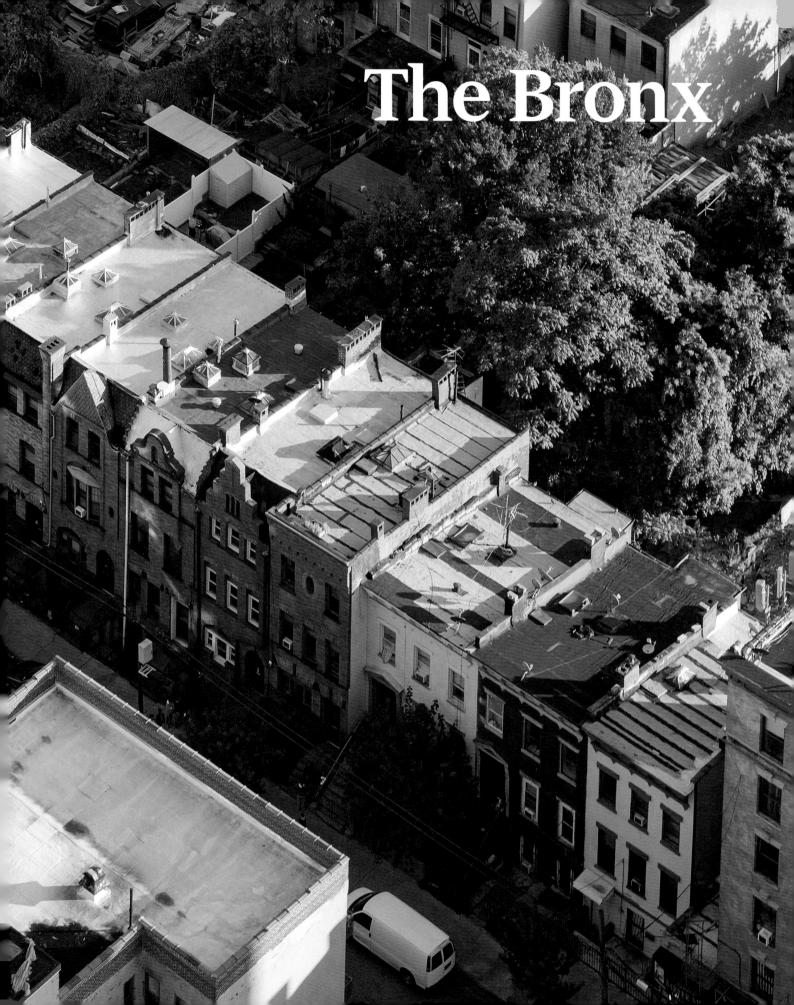

The Bronx

ABOVE East 136th Street, Bertine Block Historic District, designated 1994

OPPOSITE ABOVE East 140th Street, Mott Haven East Historic District, designated 1994

OPPOSITE BELOW Third Spanish Baptist Church (originally Third Baptist), Alexander Avenue and East 141st Street, Frank Ward, 1901, Mott Haven Historic Distric, designated 1986

PAGES 64–65 New York Botanical Garden, Enid A. Haupt Conservatory, Lord & Burnham, 1902, designated 1973

OPPOSITE AND ABOVE Astor
Court (originally Baird Court),
Bronx Zoo, Heins & La Farge,
1910–22, designated 2000

PAGES 68–69 View over the
Grand Concourse Historic
District, designated 2011

Manhattan

PAGES 72–73 St. Nicholas
Avenue, Hamilton Heights/
Sugar Hill Northwest Historic
District, designated 2002

ABOVE West 153rd Street,
Hamilton Heights/Sugar Hill
Northwest Historic District

ABOVE Hamilton Heights/
Sugar Hill Northwest Historic
District, designated 2002. Sugar
Hill Development (outside the
historic district), right, David
Adjaye, 2014

PAGES 76–77 Sylvan Terrace,
Albert Robinson Jr., 1883,
Jumel Terrace Historic District,
designated 1970

ANDREW S. DOLKART

Designating New York City Landmarks

On April 19, 1965, Mayor Robert F. Wagner signed the bill that created the New York City Landmarks Preservation Commission, the culmination of years of activism on the part of architects and architectural historians, civic groups, such as the Municipal Art Society and the local chapter of the American Institute of Architects, neighborhood organizations like those in Brooklyn Heights and Greenwich Village, critics and editorial writers, notably Ada Louise Huxtable at the *New York Times*, and scores of citizens who recognized that preserving the architectural and historical past would contribute to the dynamism of the city.

The new law established a commission with a chair and ten members who were to represent all five boroughs and professional fields such as architecture, history, planning, and real estate. The commission was mandated to hold hearings and designate individual buildings of architectural and historical significance that were at least thirty years old and to designate historic districts where the concentration of buildings created a "sense of place." The commission's authority was tempered by a major concession to the real estate industry. The time frame within which individual sites or districts could be designated was limited. The law permitted the new commission to hold public hearings on potential designations for eighteen months, followed by a three-year moratorium, after which the commission could hold additional hearings

Dyckman House, Broadway and West 204th Street, c. 1785, designated 1967 for six months, followed by another three-year moratorium, with that cycle repeated in the future.[1] Designations could take place during the moratorium, but only on buildings that had previously had a public hearing. The *New York Times* called this moratorium "an extraordinary joker" and "an ironic guarantee of speculative destruction as usual—under protection of the preservation law itself."[2] In addition, a hardship clause provided that a designation could be overturned if the owner proved that it would be impossible to generate a 6 percent return on the property and a new owner could not be found within one year to purchase the landmark. The law was amended in 1973, removing the moratorium periods and permitting the commission to hold hearings at any time. In addition, the commission was given the authority to designate publicly accessible interiors and scenic landmarks on city-owned open property. The hardship clause is still in force.

The new Landmarks Preservation Commission, led by architect and historian Geoffrey Platt as chair and James Grote Van Derpool, former librarian of Avery Architectural and Fine Arts Library at Columbia University, as executive director, held its first public hearing on September 18, 1965, considering twenty-eight individual buildings for designation. These buildings were not chosen in a void. Surveys of the city's architecture had been ongoing since the early 1940s, when Talbot Hamlin, a distinguished architectural historian and Avery librarian, compiled a list of notable buildings erected before 1865.[3] In 1951 a committee, under the joint auspices of the Municipal Art Society (MAS) and the New York chapter of the Society of Architectural Historians, expanded on Hamlin's initial list. Two years later the MAS distributed an "Index of Architecturally Historic Buildings in New York City," a list of 245 buildings or groups of buildings completed before World War I compiled by a committee of historians, architects, and neighborhood residents.

The 1953 Index established a schema—antiquity and aesthetics—by which to identify buildings deserving of protection that would guide preservation advocates and, indeed, still informs the work of the Landmarks Preservation Commission today. The list included many of the oldest surviving buildings in the city—St. Paul's Chapel in Manhattan, the Bartow House in the Bronx, Bowne House and the Quaker Meeting House in Flushing, Queens, the Billopp House on Staten Island, and various Dutch Colonial style houses in Brooklyn. Most of the other sites were structures of aesthetic significance, often representative examples of particular architectural styles.[4] Although the law permitted the designation of historically significant sites and spoke to the need to save from "irreplaceable loss" sites of "aesthetic, cultural and historic values," the commission has rarely endorsed designations for historic and cultural value alone, absent architectural significance. A more extensive list, "New York Landmarks: An Index of Architecturally Notable Structures in New York City," was published in 1957, extending the historical sweep of the survey to 1930. The introduction made it clear that these were buildings "worthy of preservation for the *architectural merit and importance, without consideration for any other historical associations.*"[5] This list was revised and expanded until 1963, when architect

and architectural historian Alan Burnham, then chair of the MAS Committee on Historic Architecture, compiled an illustrated version with 307 entries, published as *New York Landmarks; A Study & Index of Architecturally Notable Structures in Greater New York*.[6]

These lists first served as a guide for the work of the Committee for the Preservation of Structures of Historic and Esthetic Importance, which Mayor Wagner established in 1962. Headed by Platt with Van Derpool as executive director, this committee was tasked with creating a list of significant buildings and defining the parameters of a landmarks law. Between 1962 and 1965, this committee designated 3,620 buildings, expanding on the previous lists to include blockfronts of townhouses on the Upper East Side and cast-iron commercial buildings in SoHo, as well as large sections of Greenwich Village and Brooklyn Heights. Discussing some of the commission's early designations, *New York Times* reporter Thomas W. Ennis noted:

> Not all the choices are of the caliber of such obvious treasures as City Hall or its neighbor, St. Paul's Chapel. They include old Dutch farmhouses, churches, at least one synagogue, various business structures, a firehouse, Federal and Victorian homes and Fifth Avenue mansions. Some, languishing in dusty streets, will be pulled from obscurity with their identification as a link in the city's history.[7]

Made without public involvement, these designations were informal and merely honorific, since the commission had no regulatory authority. After a number of designated buildings were demolished or seriously altered, it was clear that preservation would not succeed in New York City unless the commission was empowered not only to designate landmarks but also to regulate alterations and stop demolitions.[8] The *New York Times* acknowledged that the temporary commission "has done a quietly competent job of assessing the city's past. Period by period, it has compiled lists of New York buildings for a comprehensive architectural history of the city." But, the editorial writer noted, these lists were meaningless without legislation to protect the city's architectural heritage.[9]

With the action of the City Council in 1965 and the subsequent approval of Mayor Wagner, New York joined more than seventy other American cities with preservation ordinances. Since the New York law had been passed in response

Leonard Jerome Mansion, Madison Avenue and East 26th Street, Thomas R. Jackson, 1859, designated 1965, demolished 1967

to the demolition of major buildings, the commission was tasked not only with designating buildings and districts that met the criteria of the law, but more importantly, with the authority to save those that were in danger. Now, fifty years later, it is appropriate to appraise the success of the commission in fulfilling its mandate to save endangered buildings and districts in its early years and its overall success as a force in the city.

During the six-month interval between the passage of the law and the appointment of the commissioners, demolition of the Jerome Mansion on Madison Square was scheduled to begin, prompting the *Times* to comment, "No official designation of buildings and areas to be protected can be made until the permanent Landmarks Commission is appointed. The mayor must do this . . . Until he does, the wheels of bureaucracy grind and the wrecker's ball swings."[10] Faced with this issue, at the first public hearing the commission focused on twenty-eight buildings, including the Jerome Mansion, that were in danger of being lost, rather than on the most famous or symbolic structures in the city. Chairman Platt explained that the future of the buildings selected was "most uncertain" and, thus, "the possible loss of many of these buildings was the prime factor in setting up the calendar for the first hearing."[11] Appropriately, the first building calendared was the Pieter Claesen Wyckoff House in Brooklyn, the oldest house in the city, which was in danger of being displaced for the construction of a new street. Others included the Commandant's House and former Naval Hospital at the Brooklyn Navy Yard, which the government was planning on closing; the Old Merchant's House on East Fourth Street, a privately run museum that, lacking funds, was considering the sale of the house to a developer; the E. V. Haughwout Building, a masterpiece of cast-iron construction on the corner of Broadway and Broome Street, which was in the path of the proposed Broome Street Expressway; the United States Custom House at Bowling Green, which would be vacated when the Custom Service moved to the new World Trade Center; and the abandoned former Bronx Borough Hall in Crotona Park, which some in the city wanted to demolish for park use.

The most controversial items on this initial agenda were prominent buildings that faced imminent demolition and whose designation was strongly opposed by their owners: the Jerome Mansion, which housed the Manhattan Club; the former J. P. Morgan, Jr. House on Madison Avenue and 37th Street, owned by the Lutheran Church in America; the former Astor Library on Lafayette Street, then the home of the Hebrew Immigrant Aid Society; the Friends Meeting House on Gramercy Park; the Metropolitan Opera House on Broadway and 39th Street; six buildings at Sailors' Snug Harbor, Staten Island; and the Kingsland Homestead in Flushing, Queens.

The public hearing took place during a newspaper strike so it received little publicity. But Margot Gayle, a vocal preservation advocate, was at the meeting and wrote a summary report. The meeting, which Gayle called "a sensational hearing," lasted eleven hours, with 144 people speaking in favor of designation and fourteen opposed.[12] The first official designations took place on October 14, when the commission designated twenty buildings, including the Wyckoff House, as the city's first landmark, the Kingsland Homestead, and the Sailors' Snug Harbor buildings. Designation of the Astor Library and Friends Meeting House followed later in the month, and on November 23, the Morgan and Jerome houses joined the list. In December, the commission voted not to designate the Metropolitan Opera House.[13] Thus, six of the seven most controversial items on the first calendar were designated within a few months of the initial public hearing.

Following the first designations, the *New York Herald-Tribune* published an article entitled "Twenty Buildings Saved." Frank Gilbert, secretary of the commission and later its executive director, recalls his response to this headline: "Twenty buildings designated and we had a lot of work to do on these twenty buildings before they were saved."[14] Successful preservation of designated buildings has never been guaranteed.

Even at this early date, designation of endangered buildings served exactly the purpose that proponents of the law had hoped it would, sparking campaigns to find viable uses for designated landmarks. The first building saved by designation was the Astor Library. Built in three phases, between 1849 and 1881, it had been New York's leading free reference library until its collections were moved to the New York Public Library on Fifth Avenue in 1911. The building was the headquarters of the Hebrew Sheltering and Immigrant Aid Society (later the Hebrew Immigrant Aid Society) from 1920 until the 1960s. At the time of designation, HIAS was in contract with Litho Properties, Inc., a real estate firm that had agreed to pay $560,000 for the site, where a new apartment building would rise. A lawyer representing Litho at the LPC public hearing noted that the contract contained a provision that terminated the agreement if the building became a landmark. The commission played an active role in seeking its preservation, bringing HIAS together with Joseph Papp's New York Shakespeare Festival, which announced in January 1966 that it would purchase the building and transform it into a theater center. The architect for this project would be Giorgio Cavaglieri, who, at the time, was completing the successful conversion of the Jefferson Market Courthouse into a public library.[15]

"New York City has scored its first major preservation success under its 18-month old landmarks law with the dramatic announcement of Joseph Papp's plans to purchase the old Astor Library," Ada Louise Huxtable observed in the *Times*. For Huxtable, this "miracle on Lafayette Street" had three lessons for the city, lessons that are as timely today as in 1966: first was the value of preservation as a tool for community renewal; second, the fact that without the new landmarks law there would have been no ability to explore alternative solutions for the building and no civic entity that was empowered to work for the public interest in preservation; and third, that, as she wrote, "without clients with the practical imagination and sense of historic and esthetic values to work with a landmark structure for contemporary use, the law would be meaningless."[16]

Huxtable also understood that the law could be used to "stall and maneuver" in favor of preservation, as happened with the designation of the

Kingsland Homestead. Designation gave local Flushing activists time to raise funds to move the house from its development site to a city park. At its May 1966 public hearing, the commission considered an application for a certificate of appropriateness to move the house, which was soon relocated to Weeping Beech Park and became the headquarters of the Queens Historical Society.[17] The Friends Meeting House also survives through its designation, which allowed the community time to formulate an alternative to demolition. After consolidating with the nearby meeting house on Stuyvesant Square, the Gramercy Park site was offered for development. At the landmarks hearing, a representative of the New York Monthly Meeting testified that a designation would be "tantamount to outright confiscation of the property."[18] Despite the threat that designation would be an unconstitutional taking of property and the fact that the Friends had signed a contract with a developer, the commission designated the building. In January 1967, a group of wealthy Gramercy Park area residents, under the name of the Meeting House Foundation, purchased the building for use as a cultural center. That project failed, as did the attempt by the United Federation of Teachers to adapt the building for

Astor Library, 425 Lafayette Street, Alexander Saeltzer, Griffith Thomas, Thomas Stent, 1849–81, designated 1965

RIGHT Kingsland
Homestead,
Weeping Beech
Park, Queens,
c. 1785, designated
1965

BELOW Friends
Meeting House,
East 20th Street
between Irving
Place and Third
Avenue, King
and Kellum, 1859,
designated 1965

its headquarters. The meeting house was sold in 1974 to the Brotherhood Synagogue, which undertook an award-winning restoration overseen by architect James Stewart Polshek.[19]

Preservation of the Sailors' Snug Harbor complex of five Greek Revival pavilions and a separate chapel and of the Morgan House were more difficult. The trustees of Sailors' Snug Harbor successfully sued in State Supreme Court to have the designation overturned. While the judge did not question the constitutionality of the entire landmarks law, he did rule that designation placed an undue economic burden on the property. The *Times* editorialized that the decision was "a shattering blow to the city's right to preserve landmarks of historic or architectural merit."[20] The Appellate Division of the State Supreme Court reversed the lower court's decision and the designation ultimately prevailed. After years of negotiation between the LPC, other city agencies, and Sailors' Snug Harbor, the city agreed to purchase the buildings in 1971, and they have become a lively cultural center for the borough of Staten Island. At the time the sale to the city was announced, a *Times* editorial, probably in the voice of Ada Louise Huxtable, exclaimed that "there is no longer any doubt that the concept of preservation is not only in the public interest but is a decisive factor in the quality of the environment."[21] The Lutheran Church also sued the commission for its designation of the Morgan House and won its case. This ruling was upheld and the designation rescinded. Economic conditions, however, forced the church to table its redevelopment plans and eventually sell the building to the neighboring Pierpont Morgan Library. The house was

Sailors' Snug Harbor, Richmond Terrace, Staten Island, Minard Lafever, 1831–41, Richard Smyth, 1879–81, designated 1965

redesignated in 2002 (now known as the Phelps Stokes–J. P. Morgan Jr. House).

The Jerome Mansion was the only loss among these early designations. After a lawsuit upheld the designation, the Manhattan Club applied to the commission under the hardship rule, claiming that it could not find a viable economic use for the building. The commission granted the hardship and, failing to find a new use for the building in the time frame allotted by law, gave permission for its demolition. To many, the loss of this important Second Empire style mansion, with its strong historic connections (Jennie Jerome, Winston Churchill's mother grew up here) proved that the landmarks law was flexible and was not an unfair taking of property, since an owner could apply for and be granted permission to demolish a building under the hardship exemption. But preservationist critics were less positive. In a five-part 1973 exposé in the *New York Post*, Roberta B. Gratz wrote that "commission critics argue that this is an empty boast. The Jerome Mansion could have been saved, they claim, if the commission hadn't been anxious to have that one important loss to prove to the real estate industry how small a threat they were."[22] Frank Gilbert disputes this critique and details efforts to find a new private or public user for the building, but claims that no economic use could be found at the time.[23]

Of the buildings considered at the first public hearing, only the Metropolitan Opera failed to win designation. The Met was a building of enormous importance to the cultural history of New York, but the Metropolitan Opera Company had agreed to sell the site to developers in anticipation of its move to Lincoln Center. It was clear that the commission was willing to take on powerful owners for buildings that it deemed especially worthy, but the Metropolitan Opera House was rejected. The question, then, is why did they not fight for the Metropolitan Opera House? This may be a case where the opponents, namely the socially, economically, and politically powerful board and supporters of the opera company and the proponents of Lincoln Center, led by members of the Rockefeller family, were too influential, making designation risky. The commission's first priority was preserving the landmarks law itself, and a lawsuit on behalf of the Metropolitan Opera Company would have split the cultural community and immediately thrust the young commission into a legal battle it might have lost. *New York Times* writer David Dunlap has observed that "in its infancy, the commission picked its fights with care. It did not interfere with plans to raze the 19th-century Metropolitan Opera House," quoting former commissioner Charles A. Platt asserting that the commissioners "were terribly, overly conservative in their approach."[24] Rejection was probably made easier by the fact that architect J. C. Cady's exterior was never considered especially beautiful and the sumptuous interior spaces were, at the time, not eligible for designation.

The commission held its second public hearing a month after the first, on October 19, 1965. Seventy buildings, all in Lower Manhattan, were considered, ranging from such renowned structures as City Hall, Federal Hall, Trinity Church, and the Woolworth Building, to vernacular late eighteenth- and early

nineteenth-century houses and commercial buildings. At this hearing the commission established its interest in designating sites other than buildings, hearing its first piece of urban infrastructure, the Brooklyn Bridge, and its first cemetery, the First Shearith Israel Graveyard. Before the initial eighteen-month period for public hearings had ended, the commission had held eighteen hearings and considered 580 individual sites and thirty-eight historic districts, often in marathon sessions that extended long into the evening. At the final public hearing on December 27, 1966, the commission considered a record 125 items, including eleven historic districts![25] While many New Yorkers came out to support various designations and many owners spoke in favor, there was also strong opposition to many of the designations.

Following the 1965–66 hearings, the commission designated 321 individual sites (plus 29 others that were considered individually, but were then included in historic districts) and 13 historic districts (most quite small), representing only about 60 percent of the buildings considered and two-thirds of the historic districts proposed. This initial effort reveals a great deal about the process of designation and the response to the concept of preservation. First was the issue of volume of proposed designations, which exceeded the capacity of the small staff responsible for researching and writing the designation reports. Second, the lack of political support for the commission's work in parts of the city inhibited its power. Since all designations had to be approved by the Board

Ziegfeld Theater, Sixth Avenue and West 54th Street, Joseph Urban and Thomas W. Lamb, 1927, demolished 1966

of Estimate, where each borough president had a vote, it was important to get their support. Especially in Queens and Staten Island, this was not always possible to achieve. Beginning in 1990, with the dissolution of the Board of Estimate, approval for designations moved to the City Council, where it was important to get the support of the local council member, few of whom were fully familiar with preservation issues. Without local political support, it was unlikely that a building would be designated over the opposition of an owner.

Opposition from owners has been the most significant impediment to designation. The early commissions often elected to go slowly and avoid buildings where the owner was opposed, especially if there was political resistance as well. Indeed, preservation had suddenly become a controversial issue, as Ada Louise Huxtable exclaimed in surprise: "from a safe, sentimental cause of little old ladies, landmark preservation has suddenly become a dangerously controversial subject, thanks to a law to back it up and thanks to the official designations currently in process by the city. It is a hot issue now—too hot to handle." She went on to cite some of those who opposed designation in the first two public hearings, including First National City Bank, the New York Stock Exchange, and Trinity Church and decried their lack of "civic spirit and public conscience."[26] Frank Gilbert relates that he and the commission's chairmen—first Geoffrey Platt, and then, beginning in October 1968, Harmon Goldstone—met with owners and tried to persuade them to support designation:

> We worked very, very hard to see if owners would acquiesce in the designation of their properties . . . I took pleasure in the fact, for example, that we worked out our problems with Trinity Church on Wall Street. They originally objected to the designation of Trinity Church and their related properties such as St. Paul's Chapel, and we spent a lot of time with them. We listened to them. In the end, they decided not to object to the designation of their property . . . We spent a lot of time with property owners, and we were not in a big hurry.[27]

Some buildings, such as the Old Merchants' Exchange owned by First National City Bank, were designated over opposition. But the commission avoided many other designations, including such obvious landmarks as the endangered Stock Exchange (the Exchange hoped to erect a new building), the Woolworth Building, and the original Beaux-Arts Baird Court (now known as Astor Court) at the Bronx Zoo. All of these buildings were later designated (the Stock Exchange in 1985, the Woolworth Building in 1983, and Baird Court in 2000). Some buildings languished for more than forty years—the Federal style row house at 94 Greenwich Street was first heard in 1965, but was not designated until 2009. Many others were heard, are still extant, but have never been designated. Important buildings in designation limbo were demolished, including the romantic stone Bodine Castle in Queens, Christ Episcopal Church and All Angels Episcopal Church, both on the Upper West Side of Manhattan, and 317 Broadway, the southernmost of the Thomas Twins (the northern twin is extant and has been designated as a landmark), among others. Staten Island, where political support for the LPC's work has often been lacking, has probably suffered most. In September and October 1966, the Landmarks Commission considered seventy-nine individual buildings on Staten Island. Only thirty-two of them were initially designated (fifteen have been designated since). Fourteen of the buildings have been demolished and eighteen are extant, but still have not been designated (several have been considered by the commission more than once). Of course, some of these buildings may have been considered and judged unworthy of designation, but others are major structures, including the 1763 Old New Dorp Moravian Church and a number of important mid-nineteenth-century estate houses.

Even more surprising were the major buildings that the new commission elected not to calendar. Among the important buildings demolished in the years immediately after the passage of the landmarks law were Joseph Urban's masterful Art Deco Ziegfeld Theater (1966); the Tribune Building, Richard Morris Hunt's pioneering early skyscraper (1966); McKim, Mead & White's Savoy-Plaza Hotel on Grand Army Plaza (1966); the Astor Hotel on Times Square (1967); the Singer Building, once the world's tallest structure, designed by Ernest Flagg (1968); Carrère & Hastings's Georgian-style house on Park Avenue built for former Secretary of State Elihu Root (1969); and the Brooklyn mansion of department store magnate Abraham Abraham and its two neighbors on St. Mark's Avenue in Crown Heights, Brooklyn (1972).

There are no records documenting the reasons why various buildings were not considered for designation, but it is likely that many of these were consciously avoided when the commissioners believed they would not be able to prevent ultimate demolition if confronted with a hardship application. When asked why the Singer Building was not designated, Alan Burnham, the

commission's executive director in 1967, said, "If the building were made a land-mark, we would have to find a buyer for it or the city would have to acquire it. The city is not that wealthy and the commission doesn't have a big enough staff to be a real-estate broker for a skyscraper."[28]

Instances of the LPC declining to act have marked its entire history, the most recent example being the quirky and controversial Huntington Hartford Museum by Edward Durell Stone at 2 Columbus Circle, whose facade was stripped and replaced during its conversion to the Museum of Arts and Design (2005). In many cases, including the Helen Hayes Theater, Audubon Ballroom, and 2 Columbus Circle, political pressure from the mayor made it difficult for the commission to hold a public hearing on designation.

For the most part, however, the commission has taken courageous stands, designating endangered buildings over owner opposition. Designations that were made in order to save a building from imminent demolition include Schermerhorn Row, designated in an emergency meeting in 1968; Radio City Music Hall, which the owner was about to gut prior to its designation in 1978; the Flatbush Town Hall, which another city agency hoped to replace with a parking lot; and the Coty Building, with its Lalique glass front on Fifth Avenue, which was about to become the site of a new office tower. The commission has recognized and designated buildings and districts, often in deteriorated condition, that the public was largely unaware of. This is especially true of SoHo, today one of the most dynamic neighborhoods of New York, but in the 1960s

Schermerhorn Row,
2–18 Fulton Street,
1812, designated
1968

and 1970s a backwater of aging and deteriorated cast-iron and masonry lofts. In 1973 the commission designated the large SoHo–Cast Iron Historic District, thus preventing the demolition of the largely low-scale industrial buildings and setting the stage for their adaptive reuse for housing, offices, and stores.

The commission has often gone out on a limb to designate architecturally distinguished buildings that were vacant, and in some cases had become neighborhood eyesores, with the goal of generating interest in preservation and adaptive reuse. The Association Residence for Respectable Aged Indigent Females, now the youth hostel on Amsterdam Avenue; the New York Cancer Hospital on Central Park West, now an apartment building; the Renaissance Apartments in Brooklyn's Bedford-Stuyvesant neighborhood, rehabilitated for housing; and the Flushing Town Hall, now a local cultural center, are all buildings that had been abandoned but are now neighborhood assets. Some buildings, such as the Andrew Freeman Home in the Bronx, the beautifully restored TWA Terminal at Kennedy Airport in Queens, and most of the buildings at the Seaview Hospital complex on Staten Island, are still empty, but, because of their landmark status, they remain standing awaiting new users. Perhaps the commission's most courageous series of designations was that of the exteriors and interiors of most of the Broadway theaters (with the notable exception of those on 42nd Street), over the opposition of the three principal theater owners. Following the demolition of the Helen Hayes and Morosco Theaters in 1982, a Save the Theaters group organized and pressured the commission to step in and prevent further losses. Chair Kent Barwick held hearings on the remaining theaters in 1982 and most were designated in 1987 under his successor, Gene Norman.[29]

A turning point in the designation process occurred in 1978 with the decision in the *Penn Central Transportation Co v. New York City* Supreme Court case, which upheld the designation of Grand Central Terminal and, for the first time, placed landmark designation in America on firm legal ground. The commission had designated the exterior of Grand Central Terminal in August 1967. A month later, the New York Central Railroad (renamed the Penn Central Transportation Company in early 1968) announced that it hoped to build a skyscraper above the waiting room. Architect Marcel Breuer's fifty-five-story tower design, a concrete slab faced in granite, was unveiled in June 1968. According to Breuer, the tower would "float" above the terminal, creating a "calm background" for its facade.[30] In response, the *New York Times* editorialized that "as architecture, the new tower soaring from the classical Beaux-Arts terminal like a skyscraper on a base of French pastry has the bizarre quality of a nightmare."[31] The Penn Central submitted the design to the Landmarks Commission in September, requesting a certificate of no exterior effect. Since certificates of no exterior effect are staff level permits, this was a bold move on the part of the applicant, which attempted to circumvent the public hearing process. The permit was denied. Finally, in April 1969 a public hearing was held on two possible designs: Breuer's initial proposal and a second one that would have entirely demolished the facade of Grand Central, but would have protected the magnificent interior concourse (which, as an interior, could not, at that time, be designated a landmark). Justifying this second design, Breuer stated that "there has always been some question in the minds of informed people as to whether the exterior of Grand Central Terminal is worth preserving. The best part of the present station is the main concourse, the last one of New York's great interior spaces."[32] The commission unanimously rejected both designs several months later, resulting in the lawsuit that finally reached the Supreme Court. Opponents of designation had frequently attempted to intimidate the commission with threats of lawsuits based on what they saw as an unconstitutional taking of property. With the Grand Central decision, the constitutional issue was settled and the commission was able to make decisions without fear that they would be rejected by the courts on takings grounds.

As of September 2014, just as Meenakshi Srinivasan was appointed as the

Renderings of the proposed tower above Grand Central Terminal, Marcel Breuer, renderings by Larry Perron, 1964–65

new chair of the commission, there were 1,347 individual landmarks, 111 historic districts, plus 21 extensions to existing districts, 117 interior landmarks, and 10 scenic landmarks. These numbers are far greater and the types of landmarks far more diverse than the early proponents of preservation could have imagined. Indeed, designations have been extraordinarily diverse, including favorite local buildings and monuments of world renown; tiny seventeenth- and eighteenth-century farmhouses, nineteenth-century row houses, and high-rise twentieth-century apartment buildings and hotels; commercial buildings ranging from nineteenth-century cast-iron and marble palaces and brick factories, to palatial banks and their interiors, to an Art Deco Horn & Hardart Automat restaurant, to some of the greatest skyscrapers ever built; and religious and cultural institutions of every size and style. Beyond traditional buildings, the commission has designated many small cemeteries, two trees (one has died), seven sidewalk clocks, twelve subway stations, two iron fences, three Coney Island amusement park rides, and, in one of its most original actions, the street pattern of Dutch New Amsterdam.

But still, there is much that remains to be preserved. For example, major row house neighborhoods, including large sections of Bedford-Stuyvesant and Harlem, remain undesignated; reform housing complexes such as

Amalgamated Housing in the Bronx and Amalgamated Dwellings on the Lower East Side, and important large-scale housing projects, such as the early modern Parkchester complex in the Bronx and Fresh Meadows in Queens, have not been considered for designation; and superb industrial buildings in the Mott Haven section of the Bronx and the Wallabout neighborhood of Brooklyn remain endangered. There are even some buildings that appeared on the early preservation lists that have yet to be designated. Chief among these are the Episcopal Cathedral Church of St. John the Divine; York & Sawyer's impressive Italian Renaissance palazzo built for the New York Academy of Medicine on Fifth Avenue and 103rd Street; Arthur Loomis Harmon's former Shelton Hotel, the earliest skyscraper to make expressive use of the 1916 zoning ordinance; and Helmle & Huberty's spectacular Spanish Baroque St. Barbara's Roman Catholic Church in Bushwick, Brooklyn.

Our notions of what warrants designation have also expanded. The early

Renderings of proposed tower above Grand Central Terminal, Marcel Breuer, renderings by Pierre Lutz, 1967–69

commissions designated many of the city's most venerable buildings and many of its major architectural monuments. But they were uninterested in skyscrapers. Only two—the Municipal Building and the Flatiron Building—were among the early designations. The Woolworth Building was considered at public hearings several times, but owner opposition was such that it was not designated until 1983. None of the iconic Art Deco skyscrapers were even considered. Since the early leaders of the commission came of age in the 1920s and 1930s, they were uninterested in these buildings that were only about thirty-five years old when the commission was established. The Chrysler Building was not designated until 1978, the Empire State Building in 1981, and Rockefeller Center in 1985. The designation of modern buildings would have been unthinkable in the 1960s. Yet now, after fifty years, we have begun designating buildings that were not built when the commission was established. Indeed, we now look at modern design as a historical style worthy of consideration for designation. Although most of the major monuments of postwar modernism in the city have been designated, starting with Lever House in 1982, just as it turned thirty years old, the commission has barely scratched the surface of neighborhood modernist buildings. And late modern and postmodern buildings from the 1970s and 1980s, which either have recently turned thirty or soon will be eligible for designation have not been considered at all. This includes such major buildings

New York Academy of Medicine, Fifth Avenue and East 103rd Street, York & Sawyer, 1926

St. Barbara's Roman
Catholic Church,
Central Avenue
and Bleeker Street,
Helmle & Huberty,
1910

as the United Nations Plaza Hotel (Kevin Roche John Dinkerloo & Associates, completed 1976), Citicorp Center and St. Peter's Lutheran Church (Hugh Stubbins & Associates, 1978), 599 Lexington Avenue (Edward Larrabee Barnes Associates, 1987), and Philip Johnson/John Burgee's pioneering postmodern headquarters for AT&T (1984).

In addition, the commission has always been hesitant to designate buildings based on their historical and cultural values, rather than on their architectural value. Historic designations have largely been limited to a few sites of importance to African American history, including the houses of Langston Hughes, Louis Armstrong, Louis Latimer, Ralph Bunche, and Charlie Parker, the Apollo Theater, and Weeksville. Other historically significant structures have been demolished. In 2001, the cottage on Staten Island where Catholic reformer Dorothy Day lived was bulldozed before a public hearing could be held, in spite of intensive efforts to save the building. There are no official landmarks recognizing gay, lesbian, and transgender history, or woman's history, or the importance of the Chinese, Hispanic, and other cultures in New York. No landmarks recognize the centrality of the Garment District to New York's twentieth-century economic and labor history. There are no landmarks in New York telling the story of roadside architecture, although diners, gas stations, large-scale signage, and similar structures have been recognized in many other communities.

New York's landmarks law has had an enormous influence on the character of the city, preserving neighborhoods and individual buildings that might otherwise have been lost or seriously compromised, and creating economically vital neighborhoods. The final word on the success of the landmarks law and of the Landmarks Preservation Commission goes, appropriately, to Ada Louise Huxtable, whose criticism and editorial writing in the *New York Times* in the 1960s and 1970s were essential to developing a preservation ethos in New York City. In 1970 she wrote words that are as appropriate in 2015 on the fiftieth anniversary of the passage of the landmarks law as they were then. Huxtable proclaimed that New York "has an excellent landmarks law. New York is the city where they said it couldn't happen—land values too high and real estate interests too strong and all that. Just no hope . . . The city has had some tragic losses and some miraculous rescues. But one thing is certain: there would be nothing at all in New York without the law."[33]

Staten Island

OPPOSITE Richmond County
Courthouse, Richmond Terrace,
Carrère & Hastings, 1919,
designated 1982

ABOVE Curtis High School,
Hamilton Avenue and St. Mark's
Place, C. B. J. Snyder, 1904,
designated 1982

Brooklyn

ABOVE Washington Street with
Manhattan Bridge, Dumbo
Historic District, designated
2007

PAGES 112–13 Dumbo water-
front, Brooklyn Bridge Park

ABOVE View west towards
East River and Manhattan

PAGES **116–17** Peter Lefferts
House, 1783, now in Prospect
Park, designated 1966

PAGES **118–19** Brooklyn Heights Promenade, looking west toward East River and Manhattan

OPPOSITE ABOVE Pineapple Street, Brooklyn Heights Historic District, designated 1965

OPPOSITE BELOW Columbia Heights, Brooklyn Heights Historic District

ABOVE Joralemon Street, Brooklyn Heights Historic District

PAGES **122–23** Willow Place and Joralemon Street, Brooklyn Heights Historic District

FRANÇOISE ASTORG BOLLACK

Defining Appropriateness

Right conclusions are more likely to be gathered out of a multitude of tongues, than through any kind of authoritative selection. To many this is, and always will be, folly; but we have staked upon it our all.
—JUDGE LEARNED HAND, UNITED STATES V. ASSOCIATED PRESS, 1943

Since 1965 the Landmarks Preservation Commission has been responsible for the protection of New York City's historic places, designating individual buildings as landmarks and neighborhoods as historic districts and then guiding change by applying the standard of "appropriateness." It is a complex, blessedly collective endeavor that involves the commission and its staff, preservation advocates, architects, theorists, real estate interests, neighbors, and critics. Because of these multiple points of view, the notion of appropriateness escapes dogmatism. Extracting a theory would require reconciling decisions seemingly at odds from an architectural or historic preservation perspective, but that in fact make sense in the messy reality of the city.

In the end, this collective thinking, our collective work, has resulted in a rich and varied portfolio of alterations and additions that defy simple characterizations, an object lesson in the art of design in New York's historic settings and a positive contribution to the city's urban history. I will examine this history as an architect who believes that in considering interventions to landmarked buildings or in landmark districts all approaches are valid: the only meaningful questions are "What is the right thing to do for this building, for this neighborhood?" and "What is a positive contribution from the perspective of design and preservation?"

The year 1965 was a propitious moment for the birth of the Landmarks Preservation Commission. The mid-1960s were a cultural turning point, a time when a convergence of events brought about a paradigm shift in how we saw the world around us. In particular, the publication of three books, Jane Jacobs's *The Death and Life of Great American Cities* (1961), Rachel Carson's *Silent Spring* (1962), and Robert Venturi's *Complexity and Contradiction in Architecture* (1966), questioned well-accepted orthodoxies in urban planning, environmental sciences, and architecture. Although the immediate, highly visible, consequence of Venturi's and Jacobs's work was a rush to nostalgic appropriations of the past, what came to be known as postmodernism, the intellectual and artistic developments of the 1960s had profound consequences for society's attitude to old buildings.

As the Landmarks Preservation Commission started its work, this new way of seeing layered itself upon the "old" modernist tradition, making different choices intellectually available to architects and patrons but also creating a conceptual tension between the need to be "modern" and the desire to be "harmonious" with historical settings. This tension is evident in the early debates over the Jehovah's Witnesses Dormitory in the Brooklyn Heights Historic District and the new rowhouse at 18 West 11th Street in the Greenwich Village Historic District. This tension, emblematic of the bitter architectural debates of the 1970s, surfaced again in 1989 with the addition to the Jewish Museum, but over time the commission's view, our collective view, has matured, and it is no longer engaged in an "either or" debate. In 2002, for example, the commission approved designs as different as Renzo Piano's additions to the Morgan Library and Museum and the new Congregation Edmund J. Safra synagogue by Thierry Despont.

The creation of historic districts and the approval process required for building within them have fostered a culture where new designs are debated publicly and architects have become more attentive to their building's setting. The responses are varied, and the culture keeps refining ways to build beautifully, appropriately, and well in historic districts. Since 1965, the Landmarks Preservation Commission has deemed nearly 10,000 designs appropriate to 111 historic districts and 21 extensions to districts in the five boroughs. The case studies that follow demonstrate a variety of design approaches and summarize the debate, revealing the evolving definition of a standard of "appropriateness."

Jehovah's Witnesses Dormitory and Library Facility (Ulrich Franzen & Associates, approved 1967). This was the first building to be built in the recently designated Brooklyn Heights Historic District, the first district in the city. The Watchtower Society proposed to demolish the Norwegian Club and three adjoining townhouses at the corner of Columbia Heights and Pineapple Street

RESIDENCE BUILDING
FOR
WATCHTOWER BIBLE AND TRACT SOCIETY OF NEW YORK INC.

RIGHT Perspective of Jehovah's Witnesses Dormitory and Library Facility, 119 Columbia Heights, Ulrich Franzen & Associates, 1970

BELOW Jehovah's Witnesses Dormitory and Library Facility

to build a twelve-story dormitory building. The Brooklyn Heights Association mobilized to guide the project, quickly dismissing a design by Frederic Frost and later historicist attempts by Abraham Seiden. Otis Pratt Pearsall stated the association's position: "An attempted reproduction of any historical style, whether or not found on the Heights, would not in our view enhance the District" and "It was our concept of the District that each new building should represent the finest architecture contemporary with its date of construction." In addition the association required that the adjoining rowhouses be retained and recommended that "some feature of these houses, such as the bays of those next door, might serve as an abstract theme to unite the new and the old." Finally the association urged consultation with an architect of "proven accomplishment in contemporary architecture."[1]

Franzen's design positions a new building at the corner of Columbia Heights and Pineapple Street and extends it on Columbia Street by inserting new spaces behind the townhouse facades. The height and rhythm of the old bay windows recur in a series of new splayed walls, whose angled profile is repeated in the tall corner tower. The continuous rhythm of the old bays, the new splayed walls, and the slippage of a modern plan into the historic houses blur the transition between old and new, and the tall corner tower is aligned with the larger buildings further along Columbia Heights to engage the rest of the block. The handling of the brick massing makes the building recognizable as a Franzen design, but the insertion of a modern building behind nineteenth-century facades represents an invention.

In this first application "appropriateness" involved scale, context, and architectural expression—natural concerns in any design—but the process fostered something new: the threading of old into new within a "modern" design, an unorthodox gesture.

When the building was completed in 1969, the *New York Times* observed, "Although Mr. Franzen refused to imitate or adapt any of the traditional architecture of the Heights, his contemporary design for the dormitory-library has won a Certificate of Appropriateness from the Landmarks Commission, whose first requirement for a new structure within a historic district is that it must not jar the general character of the area. Frank Gilbert, the commission's secretary, said the certificate was awarded because the new landmark in the Heights was 'a fine modern building that goes with the best of the past.'"[2]

Townhouse, 18 West 11th Street (Hardy Holzman Pfeiffer, approved 1971). The original house was part of an 1844 row of Greek Revival townhouses, but it was destroyed in an explosion on March 6, 1970—the result of unskilled bomb making by a group of political activists. The architects had proposed to set the stoop at an angle to the street wall; the commission rejected the scheme. A triangular angled bay projects out of the street wall at the parlor and second floor and creates a two-story recess for the entrance. The detailing of the brickwork supports the underlying idea: a reconstituted "historic" plane penetrated by a contemporary volume, with soldier courses on the bay but not on the "historic" plane. Clearly contemporary, the house also honors its mid-nineteenth-century neighbors through careful matching of brick and mortar and replicating the continuous cornice, the upper-story windows, and the original stoop configuration.

On May 19, 1971, after a "protracted and heated" public debate, the commission approved the design by a close vote of 6 to 5. Five commissioners feared that "the proposed design will diminish the fine Greek Revival row in which it would be located. To do so might decrease the value of the historic houses on the adjoining properties and destroy one of our best surviving entities of street architecture. We believe this to be too high a price to pay for one new house. Blast or no blast we still perceive this row as a unified composition and feel that whatever fills the hole must restore that unity or the entire street shall be diminished in architectural quality and hence value." But for the majority, "To leave the present gap unfilled is to admit defeat. To fill it with a replica of an 1844 house is to pretend that nothing ever happened here. To rebuild on the empty lot with a bold design that both respects its surroundings and asserts itself is a vital affirmation of faith in a happier future."[3]

The LPC chairman, Harmon Goldstone, favored a contemporary intervention, but the commissioners had to respond to pressures: statutory (the responsibility to preserve); political (communities groups that obtained protection for

18 West 11th Street, Hardy Holzman Pfeiffer, 1979

Rendering of 18
West 11th Street,
Hardy Holzman
Pfeiffer, c. 1971

the neighborhood would not accept what they deemed a damaging project);
and cultural (the ongoing debate between the postmodern recovery of history
and the "old" modernist outlook). The closeness of the vote in this instance
demonstrates the intensity of the debate.

Washington Court (James Stewart Polshek & Partners, approved 1984). This
complex occupies the full blockfront on Sixth Avenue between Washington
and Waverly Places. It was the first apartment building built after designation
of the Greenwich Village Historic District, and it was the subject of intense
scrutiny. As Polshek recalls, "The architect/developer–community confrontation was inevitable. Some residents testified at a community planning board
meeting that they needed the existing parking lot. Others wanted a Greek
Revival-style building or a Georgian facade, while others simply did not like the
way the building looked. I walked the streets of the Village looking for similarly
scaled projects of the past. We examined a number of Greenwich Village buildings whose roof profiles, chimney pots, and decorative detail represented an
energetic eclecticism rather than any particular style."[4]

The completed building is composed of a series of flat five-story bays faced
in brick and anchored by six-story corner towers. A sixth story is set back and
faced in a light-colored stucco providing a background against which the cren-
ellated parapets can be read. The play of figure and ground, of light and dark,
of frames and lines is used to define sub-figures in the elevation. Each bay rests
on the ground, delineating individual "houses" with frames around shop windows for individual stores. "Fitting in" encompassed not only a "compatible"
architecture but also a rhythm of use sympathetic to neighborhood patterns:
individual stores, multiple entry doors, multiple entrances, active pedestrian
traffic—a Village life.

The commission approved the project with minor changes. Roger Kimball
defended the design in *Architectural Record* by attacking "historical pastiches":
"The primary objection to the design was stylistic: it was not thought 'appropriate' for the neighborhood. Now, the wide use of the term 'appropriate' in architectural criticism these days is in need of scrutiny. For while there is no doubt
the term is often quite pertinent, it is also clear that it is infinitely malleable . . .

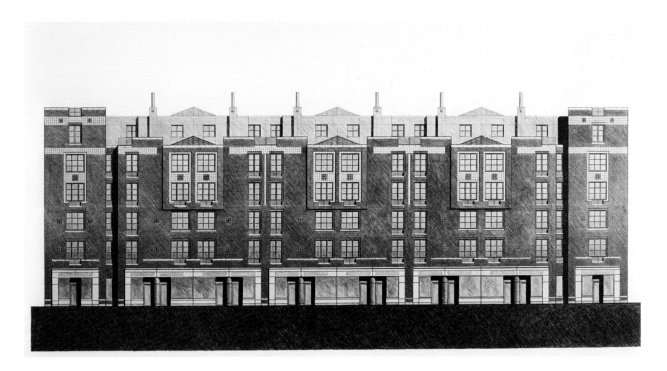

At bottom what we see in the charge that Washington Court is 'inappropriate' for its neighborhood is a reaction against its modern design that stems in part from genuine concern to preserve our architectural heritage, but also in part from a romance with historical pastiche that Postmodernism has done much to encourage."[5]

Here as in the previous cases, we see the tension between "modernity" and "history," and it is apparent from Kimball's comments that the debate is impoverished when it is reduced to such an "either/or" proposition.

Seamen's Church Institute (James Stewart Polshek & Partners, approved 1988). This project, which adds 30,000 square feet to an eighteenth-century building, was the first built in the South Street Seaport after its designation in 1977, and the commission was eager to set the right precedent: "Retaining this former chandlery of Peter Schermerhorn . . . and respecting its roof-line were primary conditions set by the New York Landmarks Preservation Commission."[6] Polshek intended to demonstrate the viability of contemporary architecture in a historic context: a new building could be respectful without being a "pastiche."

The design illustrates the architectural possibilities of additions integrated into several contexts—built and symbolic. The windows of the old building are a point of departure for the addition's window pattern, which becomes increasingly "modern" as it moves away from the original. The boundary between old and new appears to be at the parapet of the reconstituted street wall above which a new white penthouse, modern and nautical, acts as an eye-catcher. This scenographic sleight of hand resolves several issues simultaneously. The historic street wall is restated; at the same time the penthouse becomes "the

ABOVE Seamen's Church Institute, 241 Water Street, James Stewart Polshek & Partners, 1992

RIGHT Sketch for Seamen's Church Institute, James Stewart Polshek & Partners

Defining Appropriateness **133**

new," addressing the Lower Manhattan skyline. This gesture integrates the building in its immediate eighteenth-century urban context but also in the larger context of the seaport and in the emotional context of twentieth-century ocean liners with their iconic role in modern architecture. From the need to satisfy the apparent contradictions of contextual harmony and modern design emerged a visually and emotionally complex building that becomes a meeting ground for several ideas: continuity, modernity, the seaport, the larger city, the sea. Here we see the beginning of a new approach to designing in historic districts, one where "context" goes well beyond the street or the immediate neighborhood and begins to involve urban and cultural memories and iconographic references.

Addition to the Jewish Museum (Kevin Roche John Dinkeloo and Associates, approved 1989). The Jewish Museum occupies the former Warburg mansion designed in 1908 by C. P. H. Gilbert in the François Premier style. In 1963 Samuel Glazer designed an addition to the north, with a small sculpture court giving

RIGHT Jewish Museum (originally Felix M. M. Warburg House), Fifth Avenue and East 92nd Street, C. P. H. Gilbert, 1908, addition, Samuel Glazer, 1963

OPPOSITE Rendering of proposed addition to the Jewish Museum, Kevin Roche John Dinkeloo and Associates, c. 1989, building completed 1993

access to the main entrance, which was relocated from 92nd Street. In the early 1980s Gruzen & Partners designed an apartment building to replace this addition. The project was approved by the Landmarks Preservation Commission, but in the face of powerful Upper East Side community opposition, the museum decided to change course. The trustees then retained Kevin Roche John Dinkeloo and Associates to design a 30,000-square-foot expansion that could be approved by the commission and the community.

The design uses the materials and architectural elements of the original building to create a seven-story addition in the style of the 1908 building. On Fifth Avenue, the narrowness of the two added bays enhances the breadth of the original Fifth Avenue facade. The first bay is set back, keeping the original building legible, and both bays are treated in a minor key. Most importantly, the C. P. H. Gilbert building regains its historic entrance on 92nd Street, and therefore its primacy. Roche designed the expansion as if C. P. H. Gilbert had been the author. "When you analyze the nature of the architecture— height, modulation, scale, texture, the level of indentations and projections—you start to think of replicating it," he explained. "I could not see any sense in going halfway." He observed, "Only a decade ago such a post modernist solution would have been unthinkable," thereby demonstrating how much this approach is "of the moment" even though on the surface (literally) it appears to belong to

yesterday. "You could design a modern facade but what would it say? . . . The Warburg Mansion is the Jewish Museum. Anything else you'd do would make it look like an annex."[7]

Preservationists and architects were split. Charles A. Platt, chair of the Preservation Committee of the Municipal Art Society summarized the arguments in a letter to Gene Norman, LPC chair: "Those [of the committee] who favored this proposal, felt replication of the C. P. H. Gilbert design to be modest and appropriate . . . Although, perhaps artificial seeming for 1988, in an instance such as this, when the original building is of the highest quality, and the resulting replica is true to the original in scale and purity of materials, such a solution is legitimate. Committee members unable to support this request were disappointed in the proposal and felt that a great opportunity had been lost. In such instances when a brilliant architect and a client of financial means collaborate, there is the greatest occasion for a unique, creative solution of the best nature. The replica of Gilbert's original design, no matter how brilliant, is unimaginative and does nothing to show the evolution of design in our time."[8]

The commission showed no discomfort about the imitative nature of the design, finding "that the proposed addition successfully replicates the mass, details and spirit of the landmark building; that through the continuation of the landmark's architectural vocabulary a new facade of great richness and interest will be achieved which is in keeping with the character of this landmark; that recessing a 22-foot portion of the addition two feet will mark the division between old and new building; that this recess assists in articulating the relationship between the historic building and the new addition and allows the original composition of the landmark to be appreciated as an independent entity."[9] In short, the commission took a broad view of appropriateness, accepting that legibility of the addition need not be obvious; it could be subtle, available for careful study, but not overly didactic. Similarly, the commission was not dogmatic about the need for "contemporary" architecture, as it praised the architectural expression of the new design that "successfully replicates." It seems to me that the commission proved itself to be an independent thinker: while appearing conservative, it broadened the field of possibilities by declaring the design's appropriateness, giving legitimacy to its truly contemporary ideas.

Scholastic Building (Aldo Rossi, approved 1996). The first new building in the SoHo–Cast Iron Historic District, the Scholastic Building was hailed by architecture critic Paul Goldberger as "one of the most distinguished pieces of new architecture to be proposed for any New York City historic district in the last generation."[10] Located between Prince and Spring Streets, the building extends through the block from Broadway to Mercer Street. The Broadway facade picks up the horizontal lines of the Rouss building (on the south), to which it is an extension, but facade elements are scaled up. Floors are paired to form two-story groupings framed by thick white half-columns and simplified horizontal spandrels, and the tenth floor is treated as a traditional attic floor.

Scholastic Building,
Broadway between
Spring and Prince
Streets, Aldo Rossi
and Morris Adjmi,
2001

The bold color scheme also monumentalizes the design, which combines the repetitive bays of cast-iron buildings with the classical organization of masonry facades in the neighborhood. This design, however, is clearly related to Rossi's Il Palazzo Hotel in Fukuoka, Japan (1986–89), and the visual references to SoHo seem tenuous. The Mercer Street facade, however, is an invention. Here Rossi repeats a two-story element with splayed supports and structural stiffeners reminiscent of bridge structures. On Broadway Rossi remembers "the classical"; here he remembers "industry." Neither, it could be argued, is specific to SoHo. On Broadway, color is used to make the building stand out; here color is used successfully to integrate it with its neighbors.

The Landmarks Preservation Commission deliberated for less than an hour before approving the design unanimously in what some felt was a "coronation" for Aldo Rossi. For Jennifer Raab, chair of the commission, the Scholastic Building offered a "textbook example" of how to build in a historic district, as "Rossi was able to design a new facade that respected the character of Broadway but didn't inappropriately try to mimic it—and then he was more daring on the utilitarian Mercer Street facade." Not everybody agreed. Margot Gayle, the moving force behind the creation of the Historic District in 1973,

107–111 Greene Street, Joseph Pell Lombardi Architect, 2004

said, "Those large intrusive columns just don't fit, they're not friendly to their neighboring buildings."[11] (She had earlier supported the project in a letter to the commission calling it "a splendid addition to the Broadway streetscape.") But the building was well received. The landmarks law was now thirty-one years old, and a consensus was emerging about the use of historic morphologies and historic references expressed in new ways: this was becoming the benchmark of "appropriateness."

107–111 Greene Street (Joseph Pell Lombardi Architect, approved 1998). In a similar vein, this residential loft and commercial building is a refined and successful design inspired by the architecture of the SoHo–Cast Iron Historic District. As seen from the street the building appears to be five stories (the sixth and seventh floors are set back), and its street wall lines up with those of its immediate neighbors to the north and south. The three-bay facade is fabricated of riveted steel plates. Each floor is articulated by small riveted columns, supporting the broad horizontal beams, behind which is the plane of glass windows, a layering found on many cast-iron buildings. The cornice is an abstracted rendition of older cornices with steel fins as brackets. The color scheme of muted greens and dark grays adds richness to this abstract design.

The commission found that "the elegant proportions of the main facade relate well to the streetscape; that the painted steel plates proposed for the facade will evoke the cast-iron facades which define the special architectural and historic character of the SoHo–Cast Iron Historic District; that the details of the facade, including the cornice, layered columns on the facade, and storefronts, recall in a contemporary manner features found on many historic buildings."[12] The design is sure-handed and successful in its use of historical details and forms.

The Hearst Tower (Foster & Partners, approved 2001) is an addition to the Hearst Building, a 1928 design by Joseph Urban intended as the base for a taller building that was never realized. The project was proposed immediately following the attack on the World Trade Center in September 2001 and the commission approved it at the first hearing, without asking the architect to resolve formal questions raised in testimony, such as the connection between the tower and the existing building's roof. As Commissioner Thomas Pike put it, "The timing of the proposal so soon after the attack on New York would send a hopeful sign that 'the creative process' goes on in the city."[13]

The addition is a glass tower within a diagonal stainless steel frame resting on the roof of Urban's "cast stone mesa" on thin vertical columns. The landmark facade has been restored, but the interior floors were demolished to create a vast public space, an unfulfilled promise. Prior to LPC approval, the Municipal Art Society, and others, expressed concerns about the relationship of the tower and the landmarked base: "We note that the success of the design is largely dependent upon comprehending the new public plaza behind Urban's stylized and theatrical facade, and upon the public's ability to come into the space to see the tower growing out of it . . . And if the interior of the base fails to function as a real public plaza, where one can best experience the meeting of the tower and the base, the design will fall far short of meeting its ambitious goals."[14]

Before reading these comments, I saw a generic tower sitting on the Hearst Building roof on spindly legs in an unresolved transition, as many pointed out. The design was presented as a new building inserted behind the old facades transformed into screens. While one should question the enormous scope of destruction required, there could be an interesting dialogue between the existing walls and the inserted, tower, but if the tower was intended to emerge out of the original building, it should not appear to be resting on the roof. One simply wishes that the commission had taken the collective wisdom expressed in testimony and used it to benefit the project.

114–116 Hudson Street (Byrns Kendall Shieferdecker Krevlin, approved 2003). Located in the Tribeca-West Historic District, this residential project weaves a new building, built on a vacant lot, into the adjacent historic building whose facade is retained to the north. The new seven-story building contains living rooms and kitchens, while bedrooms, bathrooms, and elevator core are tucked behind the historic facade of 116 Hudson Street. The project looks smaller than it is—one is led to believe that the "new" is the modern building at 114 Hudson Street, while it also includes a new building behind the old facade of 116. In this interesting hybrid, architect and client agreed to underplay the intervention in order to achieve a better integration with the existing block. The commission paid particular attention to the new building's curtain wall and its alignment to the street wall: "the massing of the proposed building will relate well to that of the loft buildings that are typical of this historic district . . . the proportions and details of the glass curtain wall will be harmonious with the proportions, materials and articulation and streetwall of the other buildings in the streetscape and the district, which features masonry facades with punched openings." As with the Scholastic Building, the commission did not seek literal repetition of historic elements but accepted transfer of these elements into a new language.

16 West 21st Street (Morris Adjmi Architects, approved 2008). The facade of this narrow, fourteen-story residential building in the Ladies' Mile Historic District is closely related to that of the Scholastic Building, which Morris Adjmi completed after Aldo Rossi's death. Its organization of base, large middle section, and attic floor articulated with broad spandrels is a less monumental rendition of Rossi's scheme.

Here the monochrome facade is made of slumped, pressed, and carved glass, which gives the building an unexpected translucent quality—an interesting sensory overlay over the traditional loft facade design.

The commission found that "the overall development of the tripartite facade into base, shaft and crown reflects a typical pattern of facades in the Ladies' Mile Historic District; that the proposed glass facade will be a

Hearst Tower,
Eighth Avenue and
West 57th Street,
original building,
Joseph Urban,
1928, designated
1988, tower, Foster
& Partners, 2006

RIGHT 114–116
Hudson Street,
Byrns, Kendall
Schieferdecker
Krevlin, 2005

OPPOSITE LEFT
Sketch of 114-116
Hudson Street

OPPOSITE RIGHT
Detail of 114-116
Hudson Street

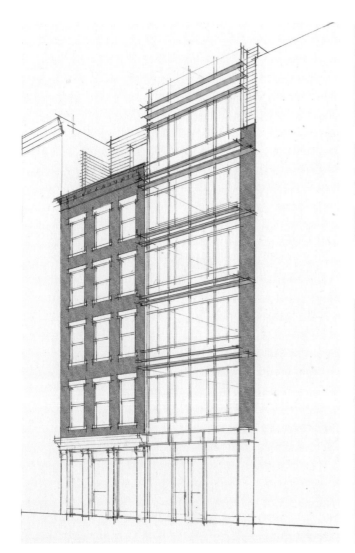

contemporary evocation of the taller historic buildings in this historic district, and molded glass will recall the features which are found on historic buildings of a similar scale."[15] While approving the design in general, the commission requested some changes at the building base to achieve a better column alignment between the base and the middle section. Appropriateness here is understood as keeping historic patterns of composition relevant through continued practice, which does not preclude a non-historic use of materials to achieve a "contemporary evocation."

What have these past fifty years of approval process contributed to our architectural culture, to our preservation culture, and to the city? Projects are now conceived, developed, and presented within multiple contexts: their immediate physical urban context, the building's historical and evolving typology, (whether commercial, residential, or institutional), iconography, and memory. According to Sarah Carroll, the commission's executive director, the "narrative has become much richer and more sophisticated."[16] Architecturally, a culture of refinement and experimentation is evolving, looking at the limits of dissonance and mimesis. Architects have broadened their vocabulary to address varied contexts. The ongoing conversation about appropriateness touches on expression, form, scale, color, materials, iconography, to name a few issues, and we have progressed from the early concern for new interventions to be "contemporary." The new work turns out to be contemporary in a different way from what we could have imagined in 1965. The work of architects in historic districts is an ongoing collective invention, a response to the city as a field of memory, realized in three dimensions, not just a physical thing but "history, geography, structure and connection with general life."[17]

The process seems to work best when the commission assumes a strong role, as it did when, in 1970, it asked that the wall of the original 1882 Metropolitan Museum building by Calvert Vaux and Jacob Wrey Mould be exposed as part of the Lehman Pavilion addition. This creative gesture put the history of the building on display, as Kevin Roche John Dinkeloo and Associates framed its rich Venetian Gothic facade with the cool monumental limestone openings of the new space's inner core. It works less well, perhaps, when the commission is less assertive, as in the case of the Hearst Building.

The conceptual armature of this collective effort is a shared belief in the value of the existing urban environment—its value as a frame for "the new," as a source of knowledge, as a library of urban history. This shared belief escapes simple theoretical definitions, and it is shaped by participants who make it evolve, adding new layers of meaning, keeping it relevant, multivalent, and fresh. This collective quality, inherent in urban environments, its lack of a single center, in time or in space, was well described by Lewis Mumford in *The Culture of Cities*: "By the diversity of its time-structures, the city in part escapes the tyranny of a single present, and the monotony of a future that consists in repeating only a single beat heard in the past. Through its complex orchestration of time and space, no less than through the social division of labor, life in the city takes on the character of a symphony: specialized human aptitudes, specialized instruments, give rise to sonorous results which, neither in volume nor in quality, could be achieved by any single piece."[18]

16 West 21st Street,
Morris Adjmi
Architects, 2009

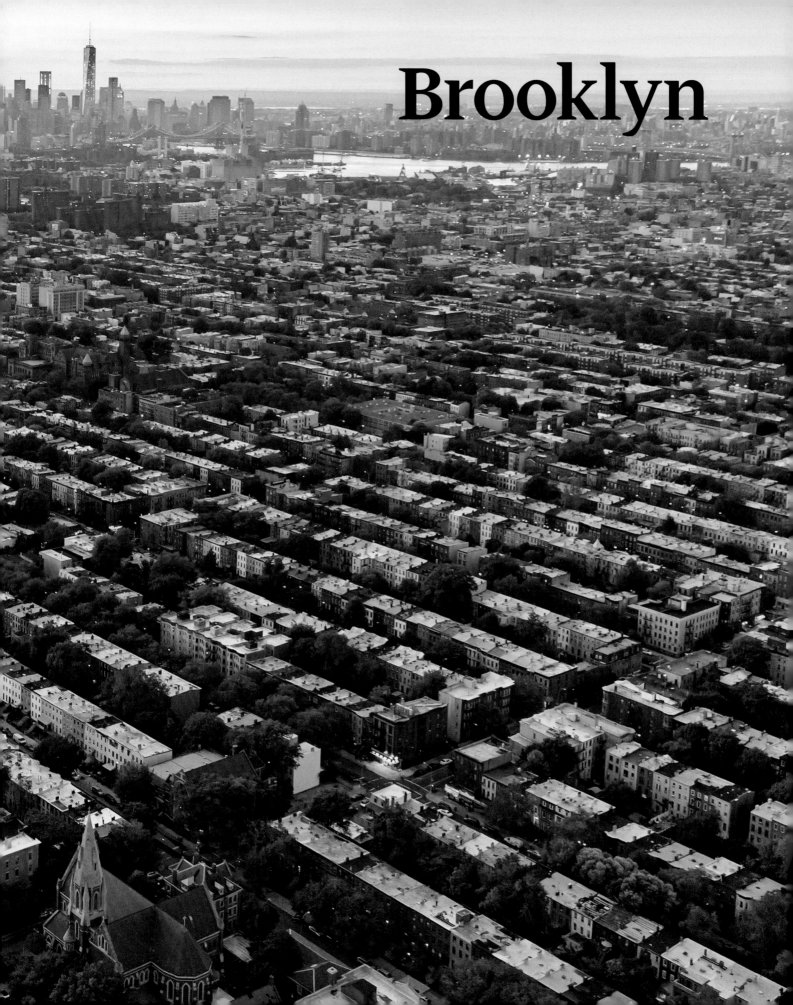

Brooklyn

ABOVE MacDonough Street, Stuyvesant Heights Historic District, designated 1971

PAGES 148–49 Bedford-Stuyvesant Preparatory High School and Literacy Center (originally Boys High School), Marcy Avenue and Madison Street, James W. Naughton, 1892, additions by C. B. J. Snyder, 1910, designated 1975

OPPOSITE ABOVE Decatur Street, Stuyvesant Heights Historic District

OPPOSITE BELOW MacDonough Street, Stuyvesant Heights Historic District

OPPOSITE ABOVE Bainbridge
Street, Stuyvesant Heights
Historic District, designated
1971

OPPOSITE BELOW Decatur
Street, Stuyvesant Heights
Historic District

ABOVE Lewis Avenue,
Stuyvesant Heights Historic
District

CLAUDETTE BRADY

Bedford-Stuyvesant: A Case Study

Bedford-Stuyvesant, originally the Brooklyn neighborhoods of Bedford and Stuyvesant Heights, has one of the largest intact collections of nineteenth-century row houses, flats buildings, and churches in the United States. The streets are lined with virtually intact Italianate, Neo-Grec, Queen Anne, Romanesque Revival, and Neo-Renaissance row houses, punctuated by the towers of imposing churches and other civic and institutional buildings built between 1860 and 1890. During that period and the first decades of the twentieth century, the neighborhood was largely made up of middle- and upper-middle-class white residents.

The 1930s brought the first of many African Americans and Caribbean Americans to Bedford-Stuyvesant, one of the few places in New York City that offered them the opportunity to purchase a home. Girls High School and Boys High School, two of the city's first public secondary education institutions, drew families to the community. Bedford-Stuyvesant was—and still is—home to many pioneering African Americans including Jackie Robinson, the first African American to play major league baseball; Dr. Josephine English, the first African American woman gynecologist to practice in the State of New York; State Assembly member Bertram L. Baker, the first African American elected official from Brooklyn; and Shirley Chisholm, the first African American Congress member. By the early 1950s, Bedford-Stuyvesant was a stable,

Grand United Order of the Tents (originally William A. Parker House), 87 MacDonough Street between Tomkins and Lewis Avenues, unknown architect, 1863, Stuyvesant Heights Historic District, designated 1971

predominantly African and Caribbean American community.

Following the enactment of the Fair Housing Act in 1968, the neighborhood began to shift. Broader opportunities afforded by the legislation, which prohibited discrimination in housing, encouraged many middle-class and upper-middle-class African American families to move to the suburbs. Simultaneously, urban renewal programs in the 1960s and 1970s replaced older buildings with government-owned affordable housing projects, contributing to more flight and displacement. Some left because their houses were taken under eminent domain; others left because they feared the new neighbors. Many of the remaining row houses adjacent to the new projects were bought by non-residents who did little to maintain them; others were abandoned and became a blight on the area.

Nevertheless, Bedford-Stuyvesant retained a significant population of homeowners committed to the neighborhood. These people worked hard, saved their money, and bought homes and futures for their families at a time when redlining was a government policy and few banks offered mortgages to African Americans. For some, financing came via the churches, like Bridge Street AME (the oldest African American Church in Brooklyn), which later formed Bridge Street Development Corporation, currently a leading provider of housing and homeowner services in the community. Residents of Caribbean descent saved through sou-sous, trust-based group savings plans made up of family and friends. The Bedford-Stuyvesant Restoration Corporation, founded in 1967, was also a source for mortgage financing. Like Bridge Street, Restoration Corporation continues to provide homeowner services as well as arts and cultural programing and education. In the 1980s and 1990s, changes in banking regulations and an increase in predatory lending practices led to more blight and displacement. Bridge Street Development Corporation's mission expanded to include foreclosure prevention services and home-buyer counseling. Churches and neighbors raised funds to save homes.

Many communities lost their best and brightest, but most of those in Bedford-Stuyvesant remained. They worked hard to stabilize the community and encouraged others to find a home in the neighborhood through organizations like Brownstoners of Bedford-Stuyvesant, Bridge Street Development Corporation, the Bedford-Stuyvesant Restoration Corporation, and the myriad of block associations and churches that all share a deep passion for this community and the well-being of its people.

The historic preservation movement in Bedford-Stuyvesant emerged from this commitment. Today there are two historic districts: the Stuyvesant Heights Historic District, designated in 1971 and expanded in 2013, and the tiny Alice and Agate Courts Historic District, designated in 2009. Recent surveys by both the New York City Landmarks Preservation Commission (LPC) and the New York State Office of Historic Preservation have concluded that an additional 8,500 buildings are eligible for designation. The Bedford-Stuyvesant community of homeowners has banded together in a campaign to expand historic district designation in the area, arguing that their homes and their blocks are as beautiful, if not more beautiful, than those in previously designated districts in Brooklyn and Manhattan.

The goal of historic designation is two-fold, the preservation of the neighborhood's built character and the preservation of the Bedford-Stuyvesant way of life. The built character of the neighborhood informs how we engage with each other. It is through the maintenance of these grand old buildings, sweeping our sidewalks, tending our gardens, shoveling snow, that we meet our neighbors and form relationships.

A prime example of community-based preservation activism was the designation of Alice and Agate Courts. Residents of these two small cul-de-sacs lined with picturesque Queen Anne style houses rallied, raised funds, hired an attorney and successfully filed an injunction to prevent a developer from tearing down the wall that marked the end of each court. At the same time they filed for designation with the Landmarks Preservation Commission, and Alice and Agate Courts became an official historic district in 2009.

Concurrent with the activities at Alice and Agate Courts, the Hancock Street Block Association started discussions about landmark designation. When we discovered that the block was part of a larger area being surveyed by the LPC, we expanded our agenda as a proposal for the Bedford Corners Historic District. With the guidance of the Historic Districts Council (HDC) we began a campaign to garner the support of the community through direct mail and community forums. Based on the response from homeowners we submitted the Request for Evaluation (RFE) in September 2008 and researched the process of designation in existing districts. One of the first things we realized was that we needed our local elected officials and residents to express their support of historic designation to the LPC.

In early 2009, armed with letters of support from each block association, we began the process of contacting our elected officials. All were receptive and sent letters of support to the commission. Our next step was to create a means for the residents to express their wish for historic designation. Taking a page from the Park Slope Civic Council, we designed a postcard for residents to sign, which we mailed to the LPC. Our local Community Board refused to support the designation process until we could prove to them that a majority of the homeowners supported designation. In the spring and summer of 2010 we started a new door-to-door campaign. First we left a copy of the HDC's "Frequently Asked Questions" booklet at every house in the district. A week to two weeks later we knocked on doors asking residents to sign a petition. We provided the Community Board with the petitions as well as statistics about how many homes were owner occupied, how many homeowners we had spoken with, and how many had signed the petition. We spoke with more than 90 percent of the homeowners, and more than 90 percent of them supported designation.

In conjunction with these on-the-ground activities, we also wanted to raise awareness about the history and architectural grandeur of Bedford-Stuyvesant within the community and beyond its borders. We held walking tours and sent press releases to the media about our upcoming meetings. Our first guide was architectural historian and Brooklyn expert Andrew S. Dolkart. His tour was so successful that we continued them, now led by Morgan Munsey, a group member and an architect, who had researched almost every building in the proposed Bedford Historic District. Additionally, we were selected for the HDC's "Six to Celebrate" program, which promotes neighborhoods whose residents are advocating for landmarks recognition. Through it all we continued to have meetings, over twenty in all, so that homeowners and residents would be well informed about the benefits and the responsibilities of historic district designation.

In its response to the letters of support from the elected officials, the LPC announced a plan to re-survey Bedford-Stuyvesant and host a meeting with homeowners from the five proposed historic districts: Stuyvesant Heights Expansion, Bedford, Stuyvesant East, Stuyvesant West, and Stuyvesant North. More than 450 Bedford-Stuyvesant residents attended the LPC meeting in February 2011. At the meeting, the commission announced the results of the survey, stating that 8,500 buildings in Bedford-Stuyvesant were worthy of landmark designation. They also announced that they would be moving forward with the designation of the Bedford-Stuyvesant/Expanded Stuyvesant Heights Historic District. Subsequently this district was designated and ratified by the New York City Council on August 23, 2011. The Bedford Historic District was calendared on January 15, 2013. Unlike the public hearing for the Stuyvesant Heights Expanded District, we had three dissenters at the LPC hearing for Bedford, all representing powerful outside real estate interests. No decision has been announced. Requests for Evaluation of the three other proposed districts are also pending.

Bedford-Stuyvesant has a changing demographic, as young people of all races discover the area. With the change in demographics and the increase in housing costs, gentrification is now the most used word in conjunction with Bedford-Stuyvesant. Almost every week, the media writes of the gentrification of Bedford-Stuyvesant, including its new restaurants and bars. What they neglect to say is that most people actively engaged in the neighborhood are African Americans. With the exception of the bars, the majority of the new restaurants and businesses are owned by African Americans. The older African American residents invested money, time, and energy into sustaining the neighborhood through the years when we were abandoned by the city and corporate America, and the media described Bedford-Stuyvesant as one of the worst ghettos in the nation.

A central debate in preservation today is the question of whether the goals of designation conflict with the goals of affordable housing. Two examples in Bedford-Stuyvesant demonstrate that preservation and affordable housing are not necessarily in opposition. Both the Renaissance and the Alhambra, two late nineteenth-century apartment buildings developed by Louis F. Seitz and designed by noted Brooklyn architect Montrose Morris, once abandoned, have been successfully converted from luxurious spaces to smaller affordable units that retain the light and character of the original architecture.

Only time will tell how the change in demographics in Bedford-Stuyvesant will affect preservation. Of the 8,500 buildings deemed worthy of designation by the LPC, only 1,291 are currently designated. Developers are constructing new buildings, and anti-landmarking interests have targeted Bedford-Stuyvesant as their new battleground. New contextual zoning has placed height restrictions on new construction on brownstone blocks, but without historic designation and its accompanying oversight, new buildings can be incongruous within the existing built environment. On the other hand, with new people and new money, we may gain new allies, those with the financial ability to fund surveys and research that can expedite the designation process.

Whatever changes may come, I will continue to work toward the designation of more historic buildings in Bedford-Stuyvesant. I wish to be like one of my mentors Arlene Simon, the Bedford-Stuyvesant born founder of Landmark West!, who organized her community and spearheaded the successful campaign to expand historic district designations on the Upper West Side.

Queens

Flushing Council on Culture
and the Arts (originally Flushing
Town Hall), Northern Boulevard
and Linden Place, unknown
architect, 1862, designated 1968

PAGES **164–65** Community
United Methodist Church,
F. P. Platt, 1923, 35th Avenue
and 81st Street, Jackson Heights
Historic District,
designated 1993

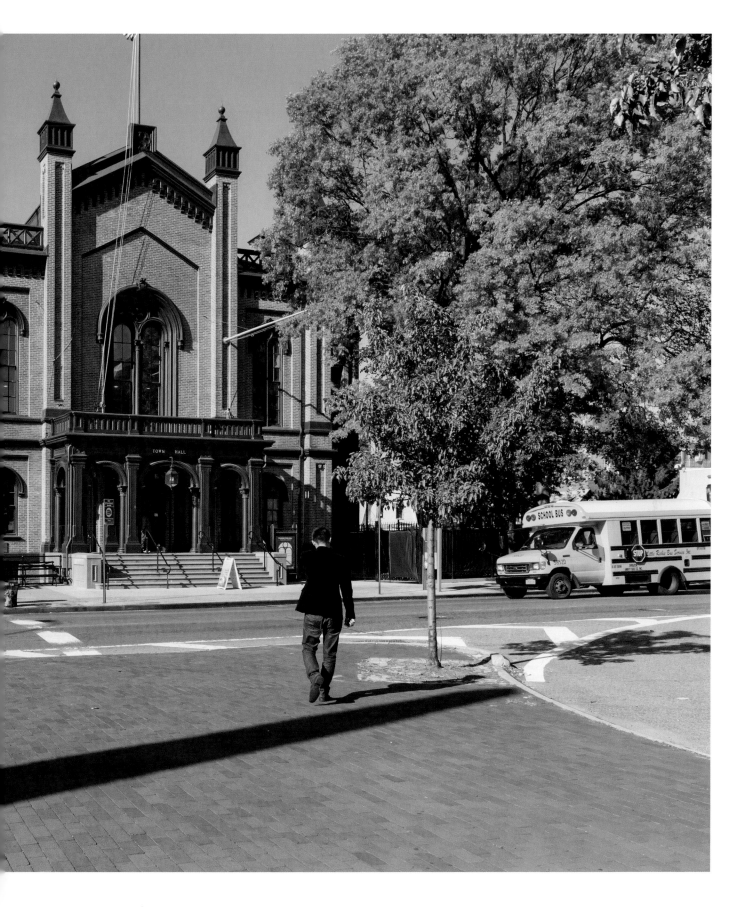

OPPOSITE ABOVE 81st Street between 35th and 37th Avenues, Jackson Heights Historic District

PAGE 166 ABOVE 80th Street between 35th and 37th Avenues, Jackson Heights Historic District, designated 1993

PAGE 167 ABOVE 80th Street between 35th and 37th Avenues, Jackson Heights Historic District

OPPOSITE BELOW 80th Street between 34th and 36th Avenues, Jackson Heights Historic District

PAGE 166 BELOW 81st Street between 35th and 37th Avenues, Jackson Heights Historic District

PAGE 167 BELOW 81st Street between 35th and 37th Avenues, Jackson Heights Historic District

ABOVE 81st Street between 37th and Roosevelt Avenues, Jackson Heights Historic District

ADELE CHATFIELD-TAYLOR

The Path Forward

For those of us who have been engaged with historic preservation in New York over the past half century, the opportunity to mark the fiftieth anniversary of the local law creating the city's Landmarks Preservation Commission is a triumphant one. In 1965, when Mayor Robert F. Wagner signed the legislation, as a country we were at the height of our losses and our helplessness. Almost no American cities had the protection of local preservation legislation, and the National Historic Preservation Act of 1966, which would help the cause all across the country, was still a year away.

As this book demonstrates, there is much to be proud of since those days, with an ever-expanding count of individual landmarks, historic districts, scenic open space, and historic interiors, amounting to almost 4 percent of the city, so that the New York City Landmarks Preservation Commission (LPC) is now "the largest municipal preservation agency in the nation."[1] This chapter will touch on the starting point of the commission and the powerful city agency it is today after fifty years of work and then speculate on what sorts of issues might confront preservation in the years to come.

Early days

History does not readily indicate the amount of the appropriation first budgeted to launch the long-awaited Landmarks Preservation Commission, but it

Manhattan, Times Square

is safe to say it was very little. Many of the eight original staff members were volunteers and standard-bearers of the preservation movement, and the chairman was part-time. In 1973, when this writer joined the staff, the law was just being amended to enable not only the consideration of individual landmarks and historic districts, but also interior and scenic landmarks. The amendment also mandated continuous hearings and actions. These changes transformed the scope and workings of the LPC and ushered in the need to expand the workforce.

In the mid-1960s the nation's first program in historic preservation was formalized at Columbia University's Graduate School of Architecture (later Graduate School of Architecture, Planning, and Preservation) led by James Marston Fitch. Students came from all over the country and from all backgrounds to develop skills in the field. *De facto,* the program generated a close-knit network of people ready to work at the LPC. Three of us were hired on the same day to shore up the regulation side of the work, interact with owners, explain the public hearing and permit processes, and generally raise awareness about the consequences and privileges of designation.

It was like working for the fire department. A call would come in, one of us would be dispatched to the trouble spot, and there we would find the offending party ripping down a designated building or doing it harm in some other way. Many offenders were completely innocent because they had not heard of the LPC, so our main job was to try to make a friend and get the situation on track.

A cherished memory of those early days was sharing an office at 305 Broadway with several magnificent women who were typing the mimeograph stencils that would later be used to run off the designation reports. Some of them had also been part of the research and writing force, but typing was the high-wire act that only they seemed capable of. If they made a single mistake, the long legal-sized multilayered templates had to be discarded, and they would have to start over. What made these women magnificent was not only their flawless workmanship, but also the fact that they had been working for years at this task as volunteers. Respect for them was instinctive for everyone from Chairman Harmon Goldstone on down; we all tiptoed as we passed through their space, lest we say or do something that would lead to the hitting of a wrong key.

I particularly remember Anne Gewirtz who, at her own expense, took the bus down from Albany on Mondays, to spend the week at the LPC typing, and there were others like her. The room felt like the city desk at the *New York Times,* with the clatter of typewriters going at lightning speed, all pushing against constant deadlines. Perfectionism was important because the credibility and professionalism of the agency had to be established at the outset, and early on, designation reports were the best way to communicate high standards. The documents were widely shared with the public, they were the starting point for the story of each property in the LPC files, and they were the legal documents that had to stand up in court, if necessary, to demonstrate that the subject met the criteria, as a building, structure, place, work of art, or other object . . . which is thirty years old or older, which has a special character or special historical or aesthetic interest or value as part of the development, heritage or cultural characteristics of the city, state, or nation.

and thereafter that the commission would see to the

protection, enhancement and perpetuation of such improvements and landscape features and of districts which represent or reflect elements of the city's cultural, social, economic, political and architectural history; (b) safeguard the city's historic, aesthetic and cultural heritage, as embodied and reflected in such improvements, landscape features and districts; (c) stabilize and improve property values in such districts; (d) foster civic pride in the beauty and noble accomplishments of the past; (e) protect and enhance the city's attractions to tourists and visitors and the support and stimulus to business and industry thereby provided; (f) strengthen the economy of the city; and (g) promote the use of historic districts, landmarks, interior landmarks and scenic landmarks for the education, pleasure and welfare of the people of the city.[2]

Besides the professionalism and prowess of these and all the volunteers, the other element of LPC life that was always memorable in those days was the public hearings. As is true today, there were two categories: designation hearings to collect testimony on properties being considered for landmark status and preservation hearings for testimony on proposed alterations to designated landmarks. Those testifying waited, sometimes all day, to articulate their points of view, and a great many of these people were volunteers, too, as those who worked full-time were not able to tolerate the unpredictable timetable.

The designation hearings, held in the Board of Estimate Chamber in City Hall, began with statements from such citizen entities as the Municipal Art Society, the Fine Arts Federation, the Society of Architectural Historians, the Historic Districts Council (established in 1971), the New York Landmarks Conservancy (1973), and the New York chapter of the American Institute of Architects, all of whom generally strove to characterize the architectural uniqueness of the subject property in the most global terms possible. It was thought that this was the most bulletproof way to protect it, and it was also the area where many of the experts were on firmest ground. These speakers, who were generally very knowledgeable, were then followed by a stream of men and mostly women, usually from the neighborhood where the property in question stood, who spoke of their own experiences of the place, whether it was witnessing Dylan Thomas sitting on the stoop in Greenwich Village holding an impromptu poetry reading on a summer evening in 1950, or watching their own child take his first steps at the Grand Army Plaza.

In general, what the community members had to say fortified the record. And at the same time, the hearings were opportunities for people to stand up and say what they really cared about, to bear witness. Each speaker seemed to be adding to an edifice that was being built before our very eyes, upon which the designation would hang, brick by brick, word by word, memory by memory, both the evidence and the argument for why people loved the city.

The preservation hearings for changes that would affect the protected features of landmarks were equally well attended, and the speakers often lingered to follow what was going on. It was all uncharted territory and fascinating to anyone who had been part of the groundswell that had taken the effort up to this point.

The atmosphere changed with the passage of the Tax Reform Act of 1976, which "provide[d] tax incentives to encourage the preservation of commercial historic structures,"[3] an avidly sought leveling of the playing field that it was hoped would make preservation as attractive to real estate developers as new construction had long been.

It worked in the sense that certain income-producing historic buildings were now looked at by developers. Preservation still attracted the amateurs, architects, history buffs, creative types, and volunteers it always had, but at the same time it became, if not overrun, at least heavily populated by people who wanted to pursue preservation so they could take advantage of the tax act. Overnight, preservation became serious business to people other than preservationists. At the same time, a whole generation of women went to work, including many volunteers at the LPC. The preservation community was shifting, adding those involved as a business venture and losing some of the old stakeholders—but this was good for all concerned as there was much to be learned from both sides.

The future

Today we see a much matured LPC with many accomplishments to celebrate as well as some persistent challenges that are growing concerns. The designation rate in recent years has accelerated, and the protected properties far exceed in number and type what the original drafters of the law expected when they presented their list of 750 worthy buildings. Today there are 31,000 protected properties, and in some areas citizens are clamoring for more. Virtually all the LPC staff members are now on the payroll, and there are many more professions represented than there were at first:

> The Landmarks Preservation Commission consists of approximately 67 archaeologists, architects, attorneys, administrators, historians, preservationists, and researchers, most of whom work in one of the agency's four departments: the Archaeology Department, the Enforcement Department, the Preservation Department, and the Research Department. The Commission also administers a Historic Preservation Grant Program and has an Environmental Review Unit that's responsible for assisting state and city agencies with the environmental review process.[4]

There is ample evidence that, after fifty years, the LPC's work is understood and appreciated. The LPC website is robust and filled with options through which a member of the public can propose a designation, see a designation report, watch a public hearing or meeting, apply for a permit, report a violation, and find specific information relating to regulatory questions and certain types of alterations. On the other hand, with 1,200 properties designated in each recent year, and more than 9,000 applications received annually from owners who wish to make changes to their landmarked properties (approximately 95 percent of which are reviewed by staff using LPC rules to determine whether the proposed work is appropriate), the workload is growing, and it is difficult to see how the volume can be sustained. Even with guidelines and master plans, the case-by-case process is time-consuming, and delays lead to frequent complaints.

No doubt in response to this crisis, the LPC announced in the fall of 2014 that it would be considering

> a proposed administrative action to issue "no action" letters for build ings and sites that are inactive and have been calendared for five years or longer (96 buildings and sites, 80 of which have been calendared for 20 years or more). This proposed action is without reference to merit and does not prevent the Commission from recalendaring these buildings and sites in the future.

The problem is that once a site has been "calendared," certain protections ensue. It cannot receive a demolition or alteration permit without notifying the LPC, which then has forty days to designate the structure or negotiate a change or withdrawal of the permit applications. Once the properties are decalendared, no notice of the application is required, and the way is cleared for decalendared properties to be altered or demolished. Announcement of this proposed "house cleaning" of the backlog caused an uproar among preservationists, so just hours before it was to occur, it was called off. But this is far from over.

On the one hand, certain communities think of historic district designation as a tool that can be wielded to stop development, and they have even been known to sue the commission to force the designation of historic districts or extensions to historic districts. On the other, the LPC is trying to deal with a large amount of unfinished business and does not have the time or resources to adjudicate each case one by one.

New York is usually in the vanguard of best practices for local preservation commissions, but given the logjam and the temper of the times, it might be a good idea for an enlightened New York foundation to sponsor a study or do a survey of other cities to discover designation and regulatory approaches that are working well elsewhere that we could learn from. Or perhaps the National Endowment for the Arts Design Program could sponsor an open, national "idea" competition for a set of new tools that could address these questions.

In addition to the changes that the LPC staff review, designation and any major changes to individual landmarks or new construction in historic districts will always require public hearings, with detailed presentations, testimony, public debate, and formal reports. So while both are definitely the responsibility of the LPC, and the present process works, it is tremendously labor-intensive, and there is no relief in sight. At the very least, the LPC needs to be more amply staffed, or the procedures revamped, or both.

Preservation and planning

The City Planning Commission (CPC) is responsible for "planning relating to the orderly growth and development of the city, including adequate and appropriate resources for the housing, business, industry, transportation, distribution, recreation, culture, comfort, convenience, health and welfare of its population."[6] It is a powerhouse of an agency, and because of its wide-ranging responsibilities, its effect on the tax base of the city, and the interest taken in its actions by the real estate community, it is of special interest to City Hall.

The Achilles heel for New York City historic preservation has long been the incompatibility, even disconnect, between some CPC policies and the LPC mandate. This reality is in high relief now as a great deal of development is in the planning stages or underway in the city, and historic areas, especially those on the edges of historic districts, are vulnerable. There are those who feel that preservation today faces greater threats than any time since 1978.

"Contextual" zoning, which determines the height, bulk, and setback of sensitive areas, "to produce buildings that are consistent with existing neighborhood character," is a relatively new and very positive option for the CPC, but vast areas of the city that clearly warrant this kind of zoning have not been updated and rezoned.

This is true in the case of the twenty-three-story development planned for the Bowlmore Lanes site, just northeast of the Greenwich Village Historic District, at University Place and 12th Street. Although the Greenwich Village Historic District has had several extensions, this part of the neighborhood remains unprotected. It is part of a two-block low-rise corridor that separates it from the SouthVillage and SoHo Historic Districts to the south, and the NoHo Historic District to the east. To the naked eye there is no discernible reason why it has not been designated on the same grounds as the rest of the area, and doing so would make the whole much greater than the sum of the parts. The value of contextual zoning in a border zone such as 12th and University is keeping down the scale of new development and thereby protecting the designated areas and low-scale neighborhood of which it is a part, even if it does not enable LPC review of the proposed design per se.

The bits and pieces approach to mapping is avoided these days, as it tends not to protect but rather undermine the whole. Neighboring historic districts (SoHo, Tribeca, NoHo, the South Village), all have extensions that include the areas that were left out in the original mapping of Greenwich Village, and these extensions have contributed to a better protected whole.

The ability to transfer development rights over individually designated landmarks has been a godsend in various cases in the city, such as saving Grand Central Terminal, but it works best if there is a market for more FAR (floor area ratio) thanks to a height limit and if the receiving site is not next door to the landmark itself, lest the additional height contribute to the landmark's disfigurement. To paraphrase the LPC's own words in refusing to grant a Certificate of No Effect to the proposal to build the Marcel Breuer building over Grand Central Terminal, there is the need to guard against reducing the landmark to the status of a curiosity: "Landmarks must be preserved in a meaningful way."[5]

Interestingly, the original draft of the LPC legislation called for a 400-foot-buffer around every individually designated building to avoid just the sort of confrontation that occurs when a landmark is smack up against a new skyscraper. That language was removed from the final draft, but it is proof of the concern over these kinds of juxtapositions, and the impossibility of recovering once they exist.

Weighing the benefits of historic preservation

Some might argue that new development is more important than preservation, but this would be an outdated way of thinking about the city. It would be useful to have a new report on exactly what landmarks and historic districts contribute to city coffers, not just when it comes to tourism, but also for what they stimulate in terms of increases to the tax base, stabilization of neighborhoods, continuity of the local culture, jobs, appeal to retired persons fleeing Florida, and so on. New development in the city is continuous and brings with it many good things, but it is important for all to know what the modest number of designated properties contribute as well.

New York takes in $55 billion annually from tourism, and surveys indicate that the city's historic buildings are the core of what visitors want to see: Radio City Music Hall, Grand Central Terminal, SoHo, Ladies' Mile District, Greenwich Village, Brooklyn Heights, Federal Hall (Wall Street), Carnegie Hall, Broadway theaters, St. Bartholomew's Church, Bryant Park, the Alice Austen House, Central Park, New York Botanical Garden, Brooklyn Botanic Garden, and the 111 historic districts and 21 extensions in all the boroughs. None of these would exist if it were not for multiyear preservation efforts, with the Landmarks Preservation Commission playing a central role in each story.

In the 1970s LPC Chairman Beverly Moss Spatt commissioned the first such study, entitled "The Economic Benefits of Historic Buildings within Historic Districts," and an update of that effort would undoubtedly reveal that landmarks and historic districts are contributing mightily to New York's bottom line and that the LPC's mission has been undervalued. There are always rumors that the LPC will soon be subsumed under the CPC, but this would be disastrous for its independence. The preservation cause is about the curatorial management of that which is already built, not about making everything "bigger and better" or reaching what is imagined to be a "highest and best use." Both agencies are responsible for real estate so the citizens are depending on them to communicate and collaborate effectively for the benefit of the city.

Options

Beyond these very big questions, there are several other issues we might think about as we mark the fiftieth anniversary of the landmarks law:

THE NEED TO KEEP GOING Preservation work is never finished. There are those who don't like the disorderliness of preservation, who are drumming their fingers on the desk wondering why we can't do the surveys, make the lists, designate the buildings and districts and be done with it. A city like New York is not a static situation. It evolves day and night and will never be finished. Worthy areas emerge over time, not only because their architectural quality begins to be of interest once their epoch has closed, but because their narrative, their story, ripens. They start to displace space in a noticeable way, and they become greater than the sum of their parts. And then the LPC is called. And the tasks that were the very first tasks to be undertaken fifty years ago are again undertaken as they will be forever: survey, designation, regulation, and education.

THE NEED TO BETTER EXERCISE THE LAW'S CRITERIA Architectural and historical significance as criteria have done plenty of service over the years, but cultural significance, something that some have found difficult to quantify or even articulate, is a concept that can and should be developed and invoked in the years to come. Had the Metropolitan Opera crisis occurred a little later, it would have qualified easily under cultural significance; similarly the Antonín Dvořák House would have been saved, and the South Street Seaport might have remained itself. The First Houses, the buildings on Hunterfly Road in Weeksville, and the African Burial Ground and Commons have been designated so there is evidence that it can be done.

THE NEED TO ANTICIPATE CLIMATE CHANGE New York is being affected by climate change, and there is already information on the LPC website about relocating mechanical equipment from basements to high positions to deal with anticipated flooding and storms. This and further information will be needed to aid the New Yorkers likely to be affected. It is also an opportunity to build new relationships with such entities as the Army Corps of Engineers, which now show an openness to new approaches (*vide* the historic town of Zoar, Ohio, which worked out a compromise to enable the historic town and a new levee to coexist). This is the perfect moment, when many agencies, at all levels of government, have to completely rethink policies and test new approaches and compromises that achieve more than one objective.

THE NEED FOR MORE PRESERVATION MODELS As a society, many Americans are uneasy with anything that is aged. As a result, the most popular model for restoration or preservation is often a multimillion-dollar campaign that makes an old building look, feel, and smell brand-new, that carefully scrapes off the patina, straightens things out, and generally takes away all the wear and tear. We need more models that show that old is beautiful, and that preservation and restoration can be modest, that it is OK to shore a building up and leave it alone so it can simply live out its life.

THE NEED TO GET MORE ARTISTS INVOLVED Artists are often the first to see potential and to bring old buildings back to life—new life—especially in warehouse and manufacturing districts that are rundown, and where prices are low. Areas in all the boroughs have been reborn thanks to artist homesteading efforts—SoHo, Tribeca, much of Brooklyn and Queens, and beyond. Because they are visual, artists see something that others miss, and they know what to do to make these beautiful old redundant structures habitable. They recognize the aliveness and beauty of oldness and know how to make these places into their homes and studios. This kind of rescue has made artists the best friends of preservationists. They have saved and transformed many buildings in New York, and now they are busy in Jersey City, New Orleans, and Detroit.

The past is an active issue, and landmarks and historic districts are living organisms that often take on a life of their own, a life that makes New York attractive to a great many people. A new study by architect-filmmaker James Sanders has found that of all the "Made in New York" tech startups in the last two decades, 86 percent chose to start in prewar buildings. Could it be that the longer we inhabit New York, the more its preexisting framework is understood to be needed for the future?

The LPC's job is to single out, designate, and protect some of the parts of the city that are exceptionally meaningful because of their age, history, or design. A lot of old buildings that will never be designated are meaningful as well. There are a great many of them, and it might make sense to designate those as "worthwhile," by LPC and CPC together, and to make them available to developers to turn into affordable housing with tax abatements for doing so. The LPC is doing a good job carrying out its mandate, but more can be done if we realize that historic preservation is in the vanguard of a new kind of progress, and that it should be more often the norm and less often the exception.

Coda

The funny thing about the fight over landmarking, whether it be Grand Central, Brooklyn Heights, Mount Morris Park, or SoHo, is that the minute it is over and preservation carries the day, for the public it is as though it never happened. There is no evidence of the struggle. The place is simply as it should be: complete, interesting, permanent.

The situation is different for battles that are not won. Madison Square Garden and the replacement of Penn Station still sicken us every single time we see them. There is so much to be grateful for, saved places that improve lives, so much that we have learned through working at it through these fifty years. What a great start for New York, and what great work lies ahead. After all, the point of all this is not to freeze New York, but to keep it alive in a way that only historic preservation can.

Manhattan

PAGES 188–89 CBS Building, Sixth Avenue between 51st and 52nd Streets, Eero Saarinen and Associates, 1964, designated 1997

RIGHT St. Patrick's Cathedral, Fifth Avenue between East 50th and 51st Streets, James Renwick, Jr., 1888, designated 1966

PAGES **192–93** Radio City
Music Hall, Sixth Avenue
between West 50th and 51st
Streets, Associated Architects,
1932, designated 1985, interior
designated 1978

ABOVE Fifth Avenue between
West 56th and 55th Streets,
showing Coty Building,
Woodruff Leeming, 1908,
glass front, René Lalique, 1910,
designated 1985, and Rizzoli
Building, Albert S. Gottlieb,
1908, designated 1985

192 Saving Place

ABOVE AND PAGES **196–97**
Carnegie Hall, Seventh Avenue
and West 57th Street, William
Burnet Tuthill, 1891, designated
1967

Manhattan **193**

Manhattan, view south to New
York Harbor

Grand Central Terminal,
Park Avenue and East 42nd
Street, Reed & Stem and
Warren & Wetmore, 1913,
designated 1967, interior
designated 1980

NOTES

Designating New York City Landmarks

1 Marjorie Pearson, *New York City Landmarks Preservation Commission (1962-1999): Paradigm for Changing Attitudes Towards Historic Preservation* (2010), 12. http://www.content. danakarwas.com/fitch/Marjorie_Pearson.pdf (Accessed August 2014).

2 "A Landmarks Law, " *New York Times*, April 27, 1965, 36.

3 The efforts to create lists of significant buildings is detailed in Anthony C. Wood, *Preserving New York*, 113–127.

4 This bias towards style in the early lists as well as in later Landmarks Commission actions was noted by Pearson, *New York City Landmarks Preservation Commission*, 1, 96.

5 Municipal Art Society of New York, "New York Landmarks: An Index of Architecturally Notable Structures in New York City," 4th edition, second printing (1957, 1961) [introduction].

6 Alan Burnham, ed., *New York Landmarks* (Middletown, CT: Wesleyan University Press, 1963).

7 Thomas W. Ennis, "Landmark Commission Seeks to Preserve Splendor of City's Past," *New York Times*, July 21, 1963, sec. 8, 1.

8 The history of the early Landmarks Preservation Commission is detailed in a Statement by James G. Van Derpool, December 3, 1964 (Avery, Burnham Collection, box 34, folder 4) and in a history of the Landmarks Commission written by Dick Williams for Harmon H. Goldstone (then the chairman of the commission), September 18, 1973 (Avery, Burnham Collection, box 34, folder 4), and is also discussed in Pearson, *New York City Landmarks Preservation Commission*, 12–15 and Wood, *Preserving New York*, 287–289.

9 "Landmarks Legislation," *New York Times*, October 22, 1963, 36.

10 "Still the Wrecker's Ball," *New York Times*, May 22, 1965, 30.

11 New York City Landmarks Preservation Commission, press release, September 7, 1965 (Avery, Burnham Collection, box 34, folder 5).

12 Margot Gayle, "Summary of the First Meeting of the Landmarks Preservation Commission—September 21, 1965" (Avery, Burnham, box 34, folder 4).

13 "Landmark Group Turns Down Met," *New York Times*, December 23, 1965, 18.

14 New York Preservation Archive Project, interview with Frank Gilbert, March 2011. http://www.nypap.org/content/frank-gilbert-oral-history-interview (accessed August 2014).

15 "A Library Ends; Move Books Uptown," *New York Times*, April 6, 1911, 1; "Aid Society Buys Old Astor Library," *New York Times*, January 12, 1920, 4; Ennis, "Landmarks for Sale"; Gayle, "Summary of the First Meeting," 2–3; "Papp's Troupe Gets 1850's Landmark for Indoor Home," *New York Times*, January 6, 1966, 25. In 1969, the city agreed to buy the building from the Shakespeare Festival which continues to operate its Public Theater here.

16 Ada Louise Huxtable, "A Landmark is Saved," *New York Times*, January 6, 1966, 25.

17 "Fund Sought to Save Landmark," *New York Times*, February 9, 1965, 39.

18 Gayle, "Summary," 3.

19 Ennis, "Landmarks for Sale"; Thomas W. Ennis, "Wealthy Group Saves Gramercy Park Landmark," *New York Times*, January 20, 1967, 71; Roberta B. Gratz, "It's Raise the Cash or Raze a Landmark," *New York Post*, May 22, 1974, 22; Ada Louise Huxtable, "Recycling a Landmark for Today," *New York Times*, January 15, 1975, sec. 2, 29; "A Happy Ending for a Landmark," *New York Post*, May 26, 1976

20 "City's Right to Save Historic Buildings Imperiled by Court," *New York Times*, May 13, 1967, 1

21 "Room With a View," *New York Times*, May 29, 1967, 17; also see "City is Purchasing Five S.I. Landmarks from Snug Harbor," *New York Times*, February 3, 1971, 39; "All Snug in the Harbor," *New York Times*, February 16, 1971, 32.

22 Roberta B. Gratz, "Are Experts Overlooking the Landmarks?," *New York Post*, January 9, 1973, 2.

23 Gilbert, New York Preservation Archive.

24 David W. Dunlap, "Enlarging the Preservation Band," *New York Times*, July 20, 1997, sec. 9, 8.

25 Greenwich Village was first heard as a single district, but was latter considered as both a single district and as eighteen separate districts (I have counted it as a single district). When the eighteen districts were considered, twenty-eight individual buildings that had been in the unified district were also heard. The commission designated Greenwich Village in 1969. The Landmarks Commission retains a complete series of its public hearing calendars.

26 "Hot Landmarks," *New York Times*, November 17, 1965, 46. Early opposition to landmarking is also discussed in Sherwin D. Smith, "The Great Landmarks Fight—Private Loss Vs. Public Gain," *New York Times Magazine*, March 27, 1966, 110.

27 Gilbert interview.

28 Quoted in Joseph P. Fried, "End Near for Singer Building a Forerunner of Skyscrapers," *New York Times*, August 22, 1967, 41.

29 The theater designations are discussed in Pearson, *New York City Landmarks Preservation Commission*, 82-83.

30 Glen Collins, "Grand Central Tower Will Top Pan Am Building," *New York Times*, June 20, 1968, 1.

31 "Jumbo Atop Grand Central," *New York Times*, June 20, 1968, 44.

32 David K. Shipler, "New Tower Sought for Grand Central," *New York Times*, April 11, 1969, 28.

33 Ada Louise Huxtable, "You Can't Win 'em All," *New York Times*, October 25, 1970, sec. 2, 25.

Defining Appropriateness

1 Otis Pratt Pearsall, co-chairman of the Historic Preservation Committee, letter to Mr. N. H. Knorr, president of the Watchtower Bible and Tract Society, December 14, 1966, Landmark Preservation Commission files.

2 Thomas W. Ennis, "Modern Building for Historic Brooklyn Heights," *New York Times*, July 20, 1969.

3 Interview of Hugh Hardy, "A Disruption in Greenwich Village," in *Historic Preservation*, July 1972: 36.

4 James Stewart Polshek, *James Stewart Polshek: Context and Responsibility; Buildings and Projects 1957–1987* (New York: Rizzoli, 1988).

5 Roger Kimball, "A Village Vanguard," *Architectural Record* (October 1986): 90–4.

6 Barry Bergdoll, "Sailors' Delight," *Architecture: The AIA Journal* (November 1991): 66–70.

7 Quoted in Peter Slatin, "Jewish Museum Expands on Fifth Avenue," *Architecture: The AIA Journal* (June 1993).

8 Charles Platt, chairman of the Municipal
   Art Society Preservation Committee,
   letter to Gene Norman, chairman of the
   Landmarks Preservation Commission,
   May 24, 1988, Archives of Friends of the
   Upper East Side Historic Districts.

9 Certificate of Appropriateness issued
   by the Landmarks Preservation
   Commission, March 20, 1989 (#89-
   0076, docket #88-2456).

10 Paul Goldberger, "Primers in Urbanism,
   Written in Cast Iron," *New York Times*,
   September 22, 1996.

11 Henry-Russell Hitchcock and Sir
   Nikolaus Pevsner, honorary co-chairmen,
   letter to Jennifer Raab, June 3, 1996,
   Landmarks Preservation Commission
   files.

12 Certificate of Appropriateness issued
   by the Landmarks Preservation
   Commission, January 16, 2002, referring
   to the public meeting of July 28, 1998.

13 David Dunlap, "Landmark Group
   Approves Bold Plan for Hearst Tower,"
   New York Times, November 28, 2001.

14 Frank Emile Sanchis III, executive
   director, Municipal Art Society of
   New York, letter to Hon. Sherida
   Paulsen, chair, Landmarks Preservation
   Commission, November 27, 2001.

15 Certificate of Appropriateness issued
   by the Landmarks Preservation
   Commission, April 10, 2008, referring to
   the public meeting of January 15, 2008.

16 Interview with Sarah Carroll, September
   24, 2014.

17 Aldo Rossi, quoted in Background
   Statement for 55 Broadway, Scholastic
   Inc., Landmarks Preservation
   Commission files, 3.

18 Lewis Mumford, *The Culture of Cities*
   (New York: Harcourt, Brace & Co.,
   1938).

The Path Forward

1 Landmarks Preservation Commission
   (LPC) website: www.nyc.gov/landmarks.

2 Landmarks Preservation Law, 1965.

3 National Register of Historic Places
   website: www.nps.gov/nr.

4 LPC website.

5 LPC report denying Certificate of
   Appropriateness to the Breuer Proposal

6 City Planning Commission (CPC)
   website: www.nyc.gov.dcp.

INDEX

ACKNOWLEDGMENTS

This book and the exhibition it accompanies have benefited from the remarkable efforts of numerous people, many of whom are acknowledged in the director's foreword. We also owe a great debt to Susan Henshaw Jones for her stalwart leadership throughout the project. Valuable contributions were made by the staff of the Museum of the City of New York: Sarah Henry offered advice and support; Susan Madden and Alexis Marion with Seri Worden oversaw a daunting fundraising effort; Julie Trebault and Fran Rosenfeld masterminded excellent programs; Noel Rubinton and Justyna Zajac headed up public relations; Jackie Zirman supervised special events; and Miranda Hambro, Giacomo Mirabella, Winona Packer, Tony Rodgers, and Lacy Schutz oversaw the registration, shipping, and installation of innumerable artifacts. We especially thank Todd Ludlam for expertly directing the exhibition's installation and Autumn Nyiri and Sara Spink for their meticulous attention to myriad details.

We also want to thank Kristina Snyder, agent for Iwan Baan, Monica Coghlan of Studio Joseph, and David Genco and Jennifer Jacobs of NR2154. Valuable conversations were had with, and advice given by, Chris Brazee, Ken Cobb, Rosalie Genevro, Frank Gilbert, Frances Halsband, Laurie Hawkinson, Jeffrey Kroessler, Jorge Ortero-Pailos, Otis Pearsall, Anne Rieselbach, Stephen Rustow, Jay Shockley, Michael Sillerman, Anne van Ingen, Mabel Wilson, Kate Wood, and Tony Wood. We also acknowledge Mary Beth Betts, Sarah Carroll, and Kate Daly of the New York City Landmarks Commission, Carole Ann Fabian and Janet Parks of Avery Architectural and Fine Arts Library at Columbia University, and Teresa M. Harris and Nicolette A. Dobrowolski of the Digital Archive and Special Collections Research Center at Syracuse University. These acknowledgements cite a handful of key people on this particular project; we need to mention as well that over our many decades living in New York City, we have continuously benefited from the advice of preservationists, architects, archivists, house museum professionals, and many more people. These stalwarts made our knowledge of New York City landmarks especially rich, an essential condition for the creation of this book and exhibition.

DONALD ALBRECHT AND ANDREW S. DOLKART

CHAIRS OF THE LANDMARKS PRESERVATION COMMISSION 1965-2015

Hon. Geoffrey Platt (1965–1968) *deceased*

Hon. Harmon Goldstone (1968–1973) *deceased*

Hon. Beverly Moss Spatt (1974–1978)

Hon. Kent Barwick (1978–1983)

Hon. Gene Norman (1983–1989)

Hon. David F. M. Todd (1989–1990) *deceased*

Hon. Laurie Beckelman (1990–1994)

Hon. Jennifer Raab (1994–2001)

Hon. Sherida Paulsen (2001–2003)

Hon. Robert B. Tierney (2003–2014)

Hon. Meenakshi Srinivasan (2014–)

PHOTO CREDITS

© Alan Schein Photography/ CORBIS **100**

American Scenic and Historic Preservation Society/Metropolitan History **45** ABOVE

AP Photo/ Harry Harris © 2015 The Associated Press **58** BELOW

Avery Architectural and Fine Arts Library, Columbia University **51** ABOVE LEFT

© Bettmann/CORBIS **46**

BKSK **142, 143**

©COOKFOX Architects **95**

©Ezra Stoller/ESTO **92** LEFT

Hearst Corp **141**

Hugh Hardy **131**

James Steward Polshek and Partners **132, 133**

© The Jewish Museum, NY **134**

Jim Henderson **99**

Joseph Pell Lombardi **138**

Kevin Roche John Dinkeloo and Associates **135**

Library of Congress, Byron Collection **49** LEFT

Marcel Breuer Digital Archive, Special Collections Research Center Syracuse University Libraries **96, 97**

Morris Adjmi Architects **145**

Morris Adjmi Architects, Paul Warchol **137**

Museum of the City of New York **44, 55, 82, 89, 92** RIGHT

Museum of the City of New York, Aaron Rose **52** BELOW, **53** ABOVE

Museum of the City of New York, Berenice Abbott **50**

Museum of the City of New York, Byron Collection **51** BELOW, **57**

Museum of the City of New York, Edmund V. Gillon **93, 94**

Museum of the City of New York, Irving Underhill **52** ABOVE

Museum of the City of New York, Philip G. Bartlett **54**

Museum of the City of New York, Simon Benepe **81**

Museum of the City of New York, Wurts Collection **58** ABOVE, **86** BELOW, **90, 98**

New York City Landmarks Preservation Commission, John Barrington Bailey **85, 86** ABOVE, **87**

New York City Landmarks Preservation Commission, Margot Gayle **56**

New York City Municipal Archives **45** BELOW

New York Public Library **51** ABOVE RIGHT

Norman McGrath **130**

Walter Daran/Archive Photos/Getty Images **53** BELOW

Watchtower Bible and Tract Society of New York, Inc. **127, 128**

Robert Walker, New York Times **49** RIGHT